Praise for *Cheating in School*

"In a high-stakes society where the ends are often valued more than the means, cheating has permeated all levels of education. This book is a must have for anyone wishing to understand the causes of cheating and find ways to prevent its occurrence."

Bryan K. Saville, James Madison University

"*Cheating in School* provides a compelling call to action. Rather than simply sensationalizing individual cases of cheating, it provides a broad and balanced perspective and outlines reasonable short- and long-term actions we can all take."

Lauren Scharff, Director of the Center for the Scholarship of Teaching and Learning (SoTL), U.S. Air Force Academy

"This book combines the work of experienced authors who have unique knowledge of different facets of academic integrity and its attendant problems. Working together, they have created a volume that brings together the various stakeholders concerned with academic cheating. They articulate the problem and define it in all its myriad forms, from the student who copies another's exam to the parent who 'helps' more than she should.

The book prompts the reader to wonder why cheating is not central to the 21st-century education agenda, and how our values become circumvented or distorted in relation to this issue."

Ken Keith, University of San Diego

"*Cheating in School: What We Know and What We Can Do,* is perhaps the most comprehensive and accessible text on the topic of academic integrity that I have read. What makes this book special is the clear intention of the authors to look beyond the individual to the broader institutional and societal milieu within which student cheating occurs, but always with clearly articulated optimism. Stephen Davis, Patrick Drinan and Tricia Bertram Gallant should be congratulated on this carefully and elegantly constructed presentation of the field."

Tracey Bretag, Editor, International Journal for Educational Integrity, University of South Australia

Cheating
in School

What We Know and What We Can Do

Stephen F. Davis, Patrick F. Drinan,
and Tricia Bertram Gallant

WILEY-BLACKWELL

A John Wiley & Sons, Ltd., Publication

This edition first published 2009
© 2009 Stephen F. Davis, Patrick F. Drinan, and Tricia Bertram Gallant

Blackwell Publishing was acquired by John Wiley & Sons in February 2007. Blackwell's publishing program has been merged with Wiley's global Scientific, Technical, and Medical business to form Wiley-Blackwell.

Registered Office
John Wiley & Sons Ltd, The Atrium, Southern Gate, Chichester, West Sussex, PO19 8SQ, United Kingdom

Editorial Offices
350 Main Street, Malden, MA 02148-5020, USA
9600 Garsington Road, Oxford, OX4 2DQ, UK
The Atrium, Southern Gate, Chichester, West Sussex, PO19 8SQ, UK

For details of our global editorial offices, for customer services, and for information about how to apply for permission to reuse the copyright material in this book please see our website at www.wiley.com/wiley-blackwell.

The right of Stephen F. Davis, Patrick F. Drinan, and Tricia Bertram Gallant to be identified as the authors of this work has been asserted in accordance with the Copyright, Designs and Patents Act 1988.

Library of Congress Cataloging-in-Publication Data

Davis, Stephen F.
    Cheating in school : what we know and what we can do / Stephen F. Davis, Patrick F. Drinan, and Tricia Bertram Gallant.
      p. cm.
    Includes bibliographical references and index.
    ISBN 978-1-4051-7805-1 (hardcover : alk. paper) – ISBN 978-1-4051-7804-4 (pbk. : alk. paper) 1. Cheating (Education) – Prevention. I. Drinan, Patrick F. II. Bertram Gallant, Tricia. III. Title.
    LB3609.D38 2009
    371.5'8–dc22
                                                                    2009007060

A catalogue record for this book is available from the British Library.

Set in 10.5/13.5pt Minion by Graphicraft Limited, Hong Kong
Printed in Singapore by Ho Printing Singapore Pte Ltd
    1   2009

Contents

Contents

About the Authors

Stephen F. Davis is Emeritus Professor at Emporia State University. In 2002–3 he served as the Knapp Distinguished Professor of Arts and Sciences at the University of San Diego. In 2007 he was awarded the Doctor of Humane Letters degree by Morningside College (Sioux City, IA). Currently he is the Distinguished Guest Professor at Morningside College and Visiting Distinguished Professor of Psychology at Texas Wesleyan University. He has served as President of APA Division 2, Southern Society for Philosophy and Psychology, Southwestern Psychological Association, and Psi Chi (the National Honor Society in Psychology). His research on academic dishonesty began over 20 years ago.

Patrick F. Drinan, Professor of Political Science at the University of San Diego, completed his PhD in 1972 at the University of Virginia, and it was there that he first developed his interest in academic integrity. Drinan served as the Dean of the College of Arts and Sciences at the University of San Diego from 1989–2007 and has been active in the Center for Academic Integrity since the mid-1990s. He has authored and co-authored many articles on academic integrity this last decade and has served as a consultant on academic integrity at the university level.

About the Authors

Tricia Bertram Gallant serves as the Academic Integrity Coordinator at the University of California, San Diego. In this capacity, she is responsible for managing the university's Policy on Integrity of Scholarship and its corresponding processes, educating the campus community on academic integrity, assisting faculty in implementing short-term cheating deterrents, and working with key campus constituencies on long-term deterrents and initiatives to create a culture of academic integrity on campus. Tricia Bertram Gallant has also been active with the Center for Academic Integrity since 2002, having served as a member of its Board of Directors and as the chair of its Advisory Council. Since completing her PhD at the University of San Diego in 2006, she has authored and co-authored many articles on academic integrity and is the sole author of *Academic Integrity in the Twenty-First Century: A Teaching and Learning Imperative*, published in 2008.

Preface

This book is a culmination of the professional and scholarly work of the three authors on the topic of student academic dishonesty and is designed to be a realistic, practical, and comprehensive reflection on the current and future states of the efforts to confront student cheating from elementary through graduate education. There has been an explosion of research and scholarship on academic integrity the last two decades, but it has not been pulled together as a compelling call for action. There have been excellent targeted books that look at discipline-based research, such as the 2007 publication of *Psychology of Academic Cheating* by Eric Anderman, of Ohio State University, and Tamera Murdock, of the University of Missouri. And, there have been comprehensive studies by UNESCO on corruption in schools worldwide but they did not give much attention to student cheating. The advantages of our book are its range across levels of education and countries, its multidisciplinary character, and the portrayal of the confrontation of student cheating as a key pivot in the reform of education: *confronting student cheating is essential to the rejuvenation of teaching and its return to a central location in our educational systems.*

Throwing light on student cheating, the "dark side" of education, is not meant as a threat to teacher morale or a blanket criticism of our educational systems. Rather, it follows the old saying that "when life gives you lemons, make lemonade." Students, parents, teachers, school administrators, and governing boards cannot tackle the student cheating problem by themselves. As you will see, it takes a highly coordinated approach by all the constituencies and stakeholders in education. This book serves as a roadmap to help those concerned about student cheating by identifying obstacles and nasty curves in the road, as well as the possibilities for desired locations at the end of the road. We even have an optimistic and provocative conclusion that speaks to finding the good in student cheating!

The intended audience for this book is large – intentionally so given the need for the broadest possible mobilization of citizens, education professionals, and students. Anyone interested in education will find useful information and fresh perspectives inside. There are many to blame in tolerating this epidemic of student cheating, but our effort is crafted so many can take credit for arresting the epidemic. Teachers, educational administrators, parents, counselors, governing boards, elected officials, and curious citizens will all find nuggets that will inspire and inform action. We hope that these education stakeholders can come together in conversation to honestly assess the state of student cheating and to innovate action to move their organizations from recognizing the problem and committing to addressing it, to institutionalizing academic integrity as a core, strategic value of the educational institution. Other important calls to action in education, such as for access, affordability, and diversity, can fall flat in the meaning they have to our schools, colleges, and universities if, once the students get there, integrity is lacking and cheating is rampant. We should not desire simply for students to get a diploma or degree, but for them to get a diploma or degree that means what it says it means.

The authors have hundreds of people to thank including colleagues, students, and, of course, Chris Cardone at Wiley-Blackwell who kept us on target. Tricia would first like to thank the students, staff and faculty at UC San Diego for their academic integrity efforts, in particular the first Academic Integrity Peer Educators (Devin, Julie, Zoe, and Yugandi) and the Academic Integrity Review Board who voluntarily dedicate their time in order to make a difference on campus. She also tips her hat to the staff and members of the Center for Academic Integrity – they are the folks around the world who recognize both the costs of ignored corruption and the tremendous profitability of academic integrity. And finally, Tricia thanks her family and friends who continue to support her work despite the time it takes her away from them; her husband, Jamie, deserves special recognition because he continues to be the best friend any woman (or writer) could wish for.

Pat developed his interests in academic integrity in graduate school at the University of Virginia and, in the mid-1990s, became active in the Center for Academic Integrity. He was mentored by Don McCabe, founder of the Center. The University of San Diego has been very supportive of Pat at both practical and research levels during the last decade. And most supportive has been Pat's spouse, Mary Ann, who has shared his interest in academic integrity during 41 years of marriage.

Steve extends his appreciation to the graduate teaching assistant who told him, "I saw a student cheating on a test today," and with that comment began a 20-year research quest to document and understand academic dishonesty. Cathy, this one's for you!

It has been both gratifying and inspiring to us that Wiley-Blackwell saw the timeliness of this book. Also inspiring has been the interest shown by parents and the public as we have shared our insights with them during conversations about the progress of the book. Virtually everyone we have talked to has shown genuine interest in our effort because it touches memories of lives in school and because people have a nagging feeling that the problem of student cheating, if not addressed, may say something both profound and dangerous about possibilities for children, education, and our common future. As a society, we often try to give voice to our concerns about what may be working in education; but there is something special and deeply personal about student cheating. Confronting student cheating is hard, but there is a promise and power in doing so that many are just beginning to realize.

Chapter 1

Cheating in Our Schools, Colleges, and Universities

A Critical Problem for the Twenty-First Century

"It's not the dumb kids who cheat . . . it's the kids with a 4.6 grade-point average who are under so much pressure to keep their grades up and get into the best colleges. They're the ones who are smart enough to figure out how to cheat without getting caught."[1]

Students from all segments of education are cheating – from grade school through graduate school, from the inner city to the country, from the poor to the rich schools, and in both public and private schools. Students are cheating because they are scared of failing. They are cheating because they are scared of having a less than perfect grade point average. They cheat on their own, they cheat with their peers, they cheat with their parents,[2] and sometimes students even cheat in cooperation with their teachers and school administrators.[3]

In this book, we explore the student cheating phenomenon, the what, how, why, when, and where of students acting in ways to "cheat" their education. However, we do not stop there with the problem of cheating. Identifying the problem is only the first step toward our goal

1

In the News

"Duke University's Fuqua School of Business announced that dozens of first-year students violated the honor code by collaborating on a take-home test that was supposed to be completed alone." This happened despite the fact that the school's honor code is displayed prominently in each classroom and students must read and sign a copy of it before they even apply to the school.

From *Inside Higher Education* (2007, May 10), "Cheating on a Different Level," by Elia Powers. Retrieved May 10, 2007, from www.insidehighered.com

---

of motivating all those with an interest in education – from students to parents to teachers to administrators – to do something about the problem of student cheating or, to be more precise, to leverage the opportunity of student cheating to make education stronger, assessment more meaningful, and the relationships between students and teachers more collegial and less adversarial. Thus, while we establish the state of the problem in the first five chapters of the book, we offer a call for action, tactics, strategies, and conversations to tackle the problem in the last four chapters.

But, before we can begin, the very first step in this discussion is to establish "what" we mean when we use the term "cheating."

Cheating can be defined as deceiving or depriving by trickery, defrauding, misleading or fooling another.[4] When we talk about student cheating, academic cheating, or academic misconduct, we are referring to acts committed by students that deceive, mislead, or fool the teacher into thinking that the academic work submitted by the student was a student's own work. Academic cheating deprives the teacher of the ability to evaluate a student's independent knowledge and abilities, as well as his or her progress in the class. Sometimes academic misconduct deprives the student of the learning opportunity intended by the teacher who created the academic assignment. And systemic and unaddressed academic cheating defrauds the public who believe that academic diplomas or degrees signify a certain level of accomplishment by the students who possess them.

The definition of cheating is dependent on expectations, and its character is marked by a lack of transparency. For example, an act, such as working with parents on one's homework, is only cheating if it was expected that the student would complete the work without assistance and if the student obscures the assistance received. As another illustration, while students are expected to write their own school papers or speeches and otherwise cite the words and ideas of others, for example, politicians are not. Why? Because the public does not expect a politician to write her own speeches (although politicians do get into trouble occasionally for "lifting" portions of other politician's speeches – see Vice-President Biden's experience with this in the 1980s).[5] However, because students receive grades for the papers and speeches they submit, and those grades are meant to reflect the student's honest writing ability and learning, we do expect students to write their own work and cite those who have contributed to their work. So, we *expect* students, for the most part, to do their own work for academic credit, and we require them to be *transparent* about the assistance they receive.

Why wouldn't students simply be transparent about the times they have received assistance if that is all that is needed to reduce cheating and enhance academic integrity? Most often, academic cheating arises out of the student's desire to produce a better product (that is, one that is rewarded a higher grade) than what she might have been capable of producing on her own. If a student is transparent about the assistance received, she might not receive as high a grade than if the teacher thinks the student did her assignment on her own. Think of the student who receives "help" from his parent on his science project or her essay; it is much more impressive when an eighth grader submits a food dehydrator as his science project or when a sixth grader submits a book report on *Moby Dick* if the teacher thinks that he built the dehydrator himself or she wrote the report without assistance.

What are the common student behaviors that belie a teacher's expectations and misrepresent the student's independent abilities in order to gain advantages?

- Working with others to come up with answers on a homework assignment when the teacher expected independent thinking and work.
- Copying or paraphrasing another's words or ideas (regardless of the medium in which the words or ideas were conveyed) without attributing those ideas or words to the other.
- Having someone else write a paper, complete homework, or take a test for oneself.
- Posting a teacher's examinations on a website or in a "test file" without the teacher's permission.
- Writing a paper using sources other than those intended by the teacher (e.g., Cliffnotes, Sparksnotes) but pretending that the assigned text was read.

In the News

Students plagiarize even though they know it is "like stealing" because they "need it," don't "feel like writing down" the source, or are "worried" about meeting the assignment deadline. Many educators think that the "cut-and-paste anonymity of the internet" teaches students that cheating is "fair game."

From *Rutland Herald* (2006, March 21), "Schools target students who think online plagiarism is OK," by Christina Stolarz. Retrieved July 21, 2008, from www.rutlandherald.com

Chapter 4 explores in more detail the different academic behaviors that constitute academic cheating. We assert that all of these behaviors, whether they are called plagiarism, copying, academic misconduct, or cheating are problematic.[6] "Really?" you the reader might be asking, "but what's the problem? Everyone does it and you can't get by without doing it." We hope that we can convince you that it *is* a problem precisely because almost everyone *is* doing it and because they think they have to do it to get by. We hope to convince you that student cheating is actually the most critical problem facing education today.

How can student cheating be the most critical problem when there are multiple other problems to worry about – dropouts, violence, drugs, underage drinking, unprotected sex? After all, while other teenage behaviors such as sex or underage drinking can have devastating personal consequences in terms of unplanned pregnancy or automobile accidents, cheating in school seems relatively benign. "Cheaters are only hurting themselves," people often argue. Or, what can cheating on one exam or one paper really hurt? And, perhaps cheating once on one term paper really doesn't matter, but then we might have to extend that same argument to the one schoolyard fight, the one-time experimental drug use, the one night of binge drinking, or the one-night stand. Academic cheating may not have the same immediate and visible consequences of these other student behaviors, but it is not without its negative consequences.

Others may argue that cheating does cause problems, but only to the cheater themself – that it is a victimless crime. People seem to be more willing to look the other way when they think that a problem doesn't affect them. Although some may argue that a brain surgeon or pilot who cheated in school can do real harm if their competence is lacking, that argument is not very compelling to most people. Who, after all, really believes that cheating on one biology quiz in sophomore year can really lead to a failure of competence as a surgeon years later? So much of learning comes from experience, after all, and there are many checks and balances so that those incompetents do not enter into critical professions.

Yet the research suggests that people who cheat are entering into critical professions because student cheating is not a rare occurrence but the normal behavior of a majority of students; as many as 74 percent of surveyed students admit to some form of academic misconduct in high school or college.[7] So, it is possible that many of our future professionals will have learned the art of cheating in school, and they learn this art in order to get into these professions.

In this chapter, we explore why cheating in schools and colleges does, in fact, pose a problem for the students as well as for the educational institution. We also discuss why, if it is so problematic, student cheating has been relatively neglected. Finally, we explore the origins of the various movements to counter cheating and how education is better positioned today to deal with student cheating than at any time in recent decades.

Concerns of Character Corruption

According to Glen Owen, an educational correspondent for *The Times* (London), a magazine survey of 2,000 mothers found that the majority of mothers admit that they "help" their children complete homework assignments and "routinely complete work to be assessed by examiners."[8] Of course, parents have traditionally been encouraged by elementary and secondary schools to participate in their children's education, so this type of behavior should not be surprising and perhaps not characterized as "cheating." If we expect it and ask for it, can we then label it as academically dishonest? Yet, at the same time, we have to wonder about the habits a child develops over time, as well as the impact of this act on the validity of the assessment process. Does a high school student who is accustomed to receiving homework "help" from his parents develop the skills and abilities to complete his work independently once in college? What is the purpose of our educational system if we are actually assessing the mother's abilities on an academic assignment rather than the student's? This simple example of "helping" on homework displays both the complexity of student cheating and the crosscutting pressures on students and their parents.

Let's examine one of the concerns hinted at in the homework helping example: that student cheating – undetected, unchecked, and unaddressed – may form a habit that persists and transitions into an adult's work and life habits. Students who persistently and uniformly complete their academic assignments in ways that shortcut effort and garner unfair advantage will learn habits of a cheating character. These children may eventually grow up to take shortcuts in life as a way to achieve personal goals, like the baseball player who takes steroids in order to beat an existing batting record or the business executive who "cooks the books" in order to artificially increase shareholder value. The Enron scandal of the early twenty-first century shows that cheaters do not just hurt themselves; they can ruin businesses, create financial and economic insecurities, and cause harm to thousands of bystanders. Persistent student cheating may corrupt a child's character and lead to a devaluing of trust, fairness, respect, responsibility, and honesty as fundamentals in a just society.

On Campus

A senior undergraduate who plagiarized the majority of a paper from various sources begged her professor and one of our authors to drop the case because she would otherwise be denied admission into pharmacy school. In other words, she was asking university employees to violate their own integrity and the school policy so that she would not have to be accountable for her choices. Do we want a student like this handling our medicine? Sure, her plagiarism might have been a one-time thing and she might eventually mature to be responsible and accountable, but perhaps a few years between her undergraduate and graduate degrees may be the time she needs for that maturing.

For many parents, teachers, and students, such a long-term vision is difficult to maintain in the face of the very real short-term benefits of cheating – higher grades that result in even greater long-term rewards such as scholarships, college admission, medical school acceptance, or a lucrative career in a top-notch firm. Grades are a commodity in our knowledge society and, to many, they represent the end goal of schooling.

Besides, cheating is relative and defined within the eye of the beholder, so aren't we just overreacting? What one teacher considers cheating, after all, may not be considered cheating by another teacher. And, sometimes student cheating accomplishes the goals desired by most of society – student graduation with a high school diploma or college degree. We can hear some readers now as we write – "Johnny didn't cheat, he was just using his resources. Don't you educators want Johnny to do well and succeed in school? You don't want Johnny left behind, do you?" The justifications for short-term or one-time cheating go beyond the self interests of the child but extend into that which we all want for all of our children – success. And, it is those short-term benefits and dreams of success that often override the long-term effects on Johnny's character, work habits, independence, knowledge, and capabilities if he persistently

---

In the Opinion of Experts

"Some children and their parents have convinced themselves that they have to be superstars and go to Harvard, Stanford, or Brown to have a worthwhile life. This attitude leads to cheating by the most qualified, not the least qualified, students in some schools."

From *Stanford Business* (2005, August), "Who says cheaters never win?" by Kirk O. Hanson. Retrieved November 24, 2008, from www.gsb.stanford.edu

"uses his resources" and short-cuts effort to get the "job" done. And, are our dreams of success really achieved when grades and diplomas are empty representations of content never learned, skills never developed, and honesty never built?

Concerns of Institutional Corruption

It is not just the disruption to a student's character development with which society should be concerned. What happens to the integrity of our educational institutions if all the Johnnys and Jennys cheat? To explore this, let's compare student cheating to something with which most readers will be familiar – driving. Most people have, at least once, driven above the speed limit, not stopped fully at a stop sign, or sped past a line of cars on the off-ramp just to cut in at the last minute. These practices, while potentially dangerous, normally do not pose great harm to one's character or others' safety. And they may, in fact, get you to your destination faster, allowing you to snag that last parking spot before the other guy gets it. Though these driving habits may be annoying to others on the road, most of us are comfortable knowing that there are laws to prohibit such behaviors and police officers to enforce those laws; we believe that, eventually, the person will get their "cumuppins" when they get caught. One could argue that even the existence of laws and minimal efforts to enforce them will deter most violators and deal with the more egregious and persistent violators.

What if, however, driving laws were defined differently on every street, resulting in a disagreement over their importance and an implicit assumption that it is acceptable to "bend" or break the laws? What if the police were reticent to enforce such laws because, when they did, they experienced political and personal backlash? How safe would driving be then? We suggest what is likely obvious at this point – it wouldn't be safe at all. There would be anarchy in the streets, particularly at crossroads where people are left to determine when and how to act. Certainly our children and pets, who we assume are

9

safe to play or walk outside on most neighborhood streets, would be in danger from erratic driving.

How is the current state of student cheating akin to this driving scenario? The rules for both are vague, often implicit, and varied by context; there is disagreement as to the importance of common standards; and most parents, students, and teachers subtly approve or support the bending of academic ethics. When schools do attempt to address student cheating, parents and students sometimes push back, like the parents of Piper High School in Kansas who convinced the school board to overturn a biology teacher's decision to fail students for cheating in her class. In protest, that biology teacher and another person concerned with the integrity of education quit and were lost to the education sector. Unfortunately for the educational system, most teachers are not like the Piper teacher – most are more likely to stay in their positions and simply allow cheating to continue.

On Campus

When "28 of 118 Piper High sophomores [who] had stolen sections of their botany project off the internet [were sanctioned] . . . parents complained to the school board . . . [and] the teacher . . . was ordered to raise the grades, prompting her resignation. Now, the community . . . [is] debat[ing] right and wrong, crimes and consequences, citizenship and democracy."

From *The New York Times* (2002, February 14). School cheating scandal tests a town's values, by Jodi Wilgoren. Retrieved November 24, 2008, from www.nytimes.com

However, we are suggesting that if parents, teachers, students, and schools continue to allow student cheating to occur and become normalized in our schools, it will corrode an essential mission of the educational institution – to develop an ethical and responsible citizenry – and undermine a useful function that schools perform for society – to evaluate and rank people according to knowledge and abilities.[9] Individual parents, teachers, and students themselves may want to believe that one-time or "minor" cheating causes little harm while facilitating a greater good – student success. The American governmental mandate of "no child left behind" would imply that success (if defined as completion of high school and entry into college) is, in fact, a major goal in America.

Success by "whatever means necessary," however, should not be. If parents, teachers, and students believe that the end (success) justifies the means (cheating) and student cheating becomes normative, the students themselves would actually be harmed in the long run. How could this be? Employers, universities, and graduate schools would no longer trust the evaluations and rankings being given by our schools, colleges, and universities. If students "use their resources" too heavily, society can no longer trust that a diploma or degree represents a certain level of independent ability and knowledge. At that point,

---

In the Opinion of Experts

David Callahan, the author of *The Cheating Culture* (2004), argued that people cheat in the world today because our society has not only failed to punish cheating, but in some ways has rewarded dishonesty. "The yawning gap between winners and losers is also having a lethal effect on personal integrity. In a society where winners win bigger than ever before and losers are punished more harshly . . . more and more people will do *anything* to be a winner. Cheating is more tempting if the penalties for failure are higher, if you're feeling pinched or under the gun . . . if the rewards for success are greater. When people perceive this kind of choice, they will often kiss their integrity goodbye." (p. 69)

cheating really has corrupted education, and the ramifications will be felt by all of society. As a result, society will not trust the education system to be fair, and economic growth, faith in business, scientific and political leadership, and a "sense of social cohesion" will be sacrificed.[10]

The Deep, Dark Secret: Cheating Corrupts Individual and Institutional Character

It is this very corruption of our students and educational institutions that is the *deep, dark* secret of academic cheating. It is deep because it runs throughout the educational system, from grade school to graduate school, and is committed by or enabled by virtually everyone involved, from students to parents to teachers to school administrators. It is dark because it represents the side of us that most possess but do not like to acknowledge – we hate cheaters but are willing to cheat ourselves in order to reach a predefined goal. And this is why it is a secret; although all of us know that cheating occurs, very few students, parents, teachers, and administrators are willing to admit its long-term negative effects and stand up, denounce it, and systematically work to address it. Nan Koehane, while president of Duke University, made national news when she used her presidential "bully pit" to announce that Duke had a problem with student cheating. Unfortunately, few others are willing to take such a stance. Christine Pelton may understand this best. She is the Piper High School teacher who resigned after her school board lacked the courage to stand up to irate parents whose children were failed for plagiarism in Ms Pelton's class.

Most often, corruption is left unchecked until the institution is hit with a message that cannot be ignored. The nationally ranked Preuss School, a charter school affiliated with the University of California, San Diego (UCSD), and the San Diego Unified School District realized this in 2007 when a grade-altering scheme scandalized the school as well as UCSD. Administrators at UCSD jumped into action by ordering an audit of the grades at Preuss, accepting the resignation of the principal, and establishing policies and procedures to inhibit such corruption in the future.

The Preuss School experience and other "cheating scandals" remind us that grades have become the goals of education, and the means of education (teaching and learning) have been compromised. And there is a sense that people are beginning to recognize the slow corruption of the integrity of education. The nature of the problem will be more fully explored in the next chapter. Now, however, we explore how we may have arrived at this state where grades (rather than learning) have become the end, and cheating has become the standard means for achieving that end. To do that, we examine two powerful phenomena that have occurred in education over the last half of the twentieth century: the rising business of education and the values wars.

The "Business" of Education

What is the business of education? In business, something is given in exchange for something else. In historical times, before the advent of currency, business was conducted by the exchange of one good or service for another. In contemporary times, we most often pay money for goods and services. What of education? In education, money (whether paid directly by the "consumer" or indirectly by the people through their government) is paid in exchange for "something else." The problematic is the varying definitions of what this "something else" is. Generally, schools, colleges, and universities conceive of money as being paid for *access* to education and *opportunities* to learn. However, the parents and children may conceive of money as paying to ensure that the student achieves "good" grades, experiences success, and receives the ultimate product – the educational credential. What has caused such disparate conceptions?

13

An International Look

"Admissions officials demand bribes to enroll . . . students, and professors expect money . . . in exchange for passing grades. The black-market pipeline of money and perks thrives even as the system itself is eroding . . . A poll last year by Transparency International . . . found that 66 percent of Russians consider the higher-education system to be corrupt."

From *Chronicle of Higher Education* (2008, February 22), "In Russia, corruption plagues the higher education system," by Anna Nemtsova. Retrieved February 22, 2008, from www.chronicle.com

The value of an educational credential, as well as its meaning within society, has been substantially altered along with the altering of the economy from one that was agriculture-based, to one that was industry-based and now to one that is knowledge-based. An educational credential is no longer considered a luxury or of limited utility (that is, only for certain professions such as teachers, lawyers, and doctors). Beginning in the twentieth century, and certainly into the twenty-first century, education blossomed into a human right, and the educational credential became anchored in our economy as a necessity for the majority of workers.[11] The possession of a college diploma or university degree has become epitomized as the prerequisite for achieving the American dream (Bill Gates excluded). In fact, the educational credential is quickly becoming a prerequisite for the "American dream" (qualified as financial security, home ownership, gainful employment) in many societies beyond the western world – certainly those which are major players in the world economy, with China and India as the most notable (see the box above and on the next page). The educational degree as requisite has amplified the business of education.

An International Look

In China, the "gaokao" is the national university entrance exam, one "seen as key to social mobility – the best chance for school-leavers to land white-collar jobs." As a result of the importance of the gaokao, and the stress that it causes, "stories of cheating surface every year, despite stiff penalties. Students reportedly pay for leaked exam papers, smuggle in mobile phones and electronic dictionaries, or pay others to take the exam for them."

From *Reuters* (2008, June 6). "Factbox: China's dreaded 'gaokao,' the world's largest exam," by Guo Shipeng and Gillian Murdoch. Retrieved November 24, 2008, from www.reuters.com

---

Why would this be the case? When education is a requisite, as it is in most developed countries, the government dedicates significant and growing financial resources.[12] The pressure to pour more resources into education has rightly fueled demands for greater accountability and choice. The public wants to ensure that they are getting "something" for their investment, and that induces the necessity of measuring and evaluating those "somethings." This, then, spreads the business of education beyond private schools that are tuition-based to public schools – each of us pays for schooling and thus demands something in return. And, with increased measurements and evaluations, there are increased opportunities for corruption. This argument is supported by a massive international study backed by the United Nations Educational, Scientific and Cultural Organization (UNESCO) entitled *Corrupt Schools, Corrupt Universities: What Can Be Done?* The authors of the study, Jacques Hallak and Muriel Poisson, reviewed patterns of corruption worldwide in education and found a myriad of ways that corruption occurs from contract kickbacks to nepotism to falsification of

15

records to private tutoring abuses.[13] Through their work, Hallak and Poisson demonstrated that corruption can be found almost everywhere in educational systems, thus requiring strenuous efforts at transparency and accountability.

The business side of education may invite blatant administrative and teacher corruption which can desecrate the meaning and value of an educational credential. However, others worry that the move of schools, colleges, and universities to be more "commercial" undermines a focus on teaching and learning.[14] In the K-12 system, the commercial market is becoming increasingly involved, whether it be through donations and grants or in arrangements to deliver products to a captive group of consumers.[15] In the postsecondary education system, it has been argued that less attention is paid to teaching, learning, and the construction of knowledge as increased attention is paid to "products" developed through research, service, sports, and entertainment.[16]

In the News

"Spending on education now accounts for a larger share of the gross domestic product than any other service sector except healthcare. The No Child Left Behind Law ... is one of the reasons ... [because it] requires frequent testing of students ... to measure their progress ... [and] that's ... a big boost to ... standardized tests [firms]."

From the PBS Nightly Business Report (February 18, 2008), "The new business of education – standardized testing," quoting Susie Gharib

---

An illustrative example of this trend can be found at Kansas State University where, in April of 2008, the athletic program was moved under the Vice-President for Advancement – the person charged with raising money for the university. This move has two implications: (1) it suggests that the athletic program is distinguished more as a business opportunity and less as a component of the teaching and learning environment; and (2) the main fundraiser for the university should pay more attention to the monetary needs of the athletic teams than of the teachers and students in the classroom. In *University Inc.: The Corporate Corruption of American Higher Education*, Jennifer Washburn argues that the "great strength" of education is "in its capacity to appreciate the intrinsic value of intellectual discovery, human creativity, knowledge, and ideas."[17] If education becomes preoccupied with short-term economic payoffs, there will be less emphasis on teaching and basic research, and education will "be surrendered to the narrow dictates of the market."[18]

The shift in focus away from teaching is also somewhat represented by the simultaneous reduction of full-time faculty while the use of part-time faculty and creation of noninstructional areas (e.g., research and public service) grow within educational organizations.[19] The increased profile of administrators has been driven, in part, by legal mandates to address everything from special education to sexual harassment, but also by the commercialization of education. Even public safety on campuses has generated its own professional and credentialing associations!

In the News

"In the past 30 years, part-time faculty at US colleges and universities has jumped from 22 percent to 43 percent ... [and] these instructors ... make 40 cents on the dollar compared with full-time faculty ... But with the prospect of tighter college and university budgets ahead, the use of part-time faculty is likely to grow."

From *Education Watch* (2003, February 7), "Growing use of adjunct professors sparks debate and push for change," by Caralee Adams. Retrieved November 24, 2008, from www.aarp.org

---

There are some valid reasons to increase management and administrative staff; after all, "teachable moments" do not just occur in the classroom but in all interactions and experiences students have within the institution. The expansion of the student affairs profession in postsecondary education in America over the twentieth century provides one of the most illustrative examples of this phenomenon. Colleges and universities around the world are now emulating the growth of student affairs administration; University of California, San Diego, for example, hosted administrators and scholars from several Chinese universities in the fall of 2008 who were visiting to learn more about the practice of student affairs administration in America. However beneficial the growth of student affairs and other administrative professionals may be, it is important also to understand that the scale and growth of new layers of administration have focused resources away from classroom instruction at all levels of education.[20] While administrative positions have been created, full-time instructional positions have remained steady or decreased, and all the while class sizes have continued to increase.[21]

Class sizes do not simply increase within the confines of the physical classroom (which would eventually restrict the number of enrollees). Technologies have helped to commercialize education by enabling huge economies of scale through web-based instruction.[22] The shape of this initiative has foreseeable and unforeseeable aspects. Obviously, resources to support the information revolution will be needed, and new managerial elites and technocrats will be hired to shepherd the process. Meanwhile, the power of the information revolution and ease of access to information may sway the public that computer literacy may be the only literacy needed. Yet others caution that computer literacy will not be a sufficient skill for resolving the critical problems facing the world in the twenty-first century (e.g., poverty, global warming).

The full consequences of the information revolution associated with computer technology will take several decades to unfold, and the unintended ones are likely to be surprising and deep. We do know some of the immediate consequences, however, in the proliferation of opportunities for cheating and the hints of shifts in ways the younger generations view knowledge construction, information, and culture as property. The fight between the music industry and the young people who download music for free provides one illustration of the complications that have emerged from the information revolution (see the box below). (More on the impact of technology on the problem of student cheating in the next chapter.)

In the News

"Colleges are finding themselves in the middle . . . between the recording and movie industries on one side and computer users [who] download copyrighted works for free, on the other . . . [Representatives from] universities and business implied that ratcheting up their policing mechanisms in response to every new innovation by peer-to-peer networks was ultimately unsustainable."

From *Inside Higher Education* (2007, June 6), "Sharing ideas about sharing files" by Andy Guess. Retrieved June 6, 2007, from www.insidehighered.com

---

The business of education has supplied ample distractions in emphasizing success, competition, results, and credentials. These are not, in themselves, negative except to the extent that they push out integrity as a central preoccupation. The stakes of education seem much higher now, and cutting corners to achieve higher grades than one deserves can be a greater temptation than before. Even the trend of grade inflation has not dampened the temptation and may have even accelerated it by suggesting that grades are just formalities that can be adjusted upward for no better reason than an emphasis of rewards over penalties.

19

Interestingly, grade inflation is an important inflection point in the understanding of how serious the matter of student cheating has become in education. At first glance, one would expect that grade inflation would take pressure off students in their ambition for higher grades and thus diminish incentives to cheat. Whatever the causes and intentions associated with generally increased grade levels, a perverse and unintended consequence may have been to increase incentives to cheat. Grade inflation signals to students that high grades are important, expected, and normal; therefore, pressure to achieve high grades actually increases rather than decreases incentives to cheat. Excuses for poor performance are less credible, and the Lake Woebegone effect – everyone is above average – pushes students to meet expectations by cutting corners, as seen in the quote at the beginning of this chapter. Educators themselves seem confounded by this phenomenon as they spend more time worrying about assessment and testing rather than the gap between higher grades and modest evidence of genuine achievement. And, of course, pressure on teachers and schools worldwide to show testing success has increased incentives for cutting corners not only by teaching to the test but also through corruption in grading and compilation of results.[23]

In the Opinion of Experts

Grade inflation "differentiates among students less and gives them less feedback on the quality of the work . . . [so] it's generally a disincentive for working harder because it really means it's easier to get a higher grade . . . [and it gives students] an inflated view of themselves in terms of . . . what they can do academically."

From *The Journal, Queens University* (2008, September 19), "Making the grade: Standard tests could solve grade inflation problem, expert says," by Michael Woods. Retrieved November 15, 2008, from www.queensjournal.ca

The business of education has actually increased possibilities of corruption, including student cheating, but we need not be fatalistic about it. All institutions in a society need to adapt to new situations. All institutions pay attention to their own coherence and survival. Businesses themselves know the importance of brand integrity and invest heavily to protect and defend it. Of course, businesses have been encouraged to support and brand integrity by such federal legislation as the Sarbanes-Oxley Act and laws such as the Federal Sentencing Guidelines for Organizations, both of which mandate organizations to enhance organizational ethics through implementation of ethics codes, ethics training, and sanctions for misconduct.[24] Education, perhaps even more than businesses, ought to be attentive to branding integrity, even if external pressure is lacking. It is the educational system, after all, in which those leading and managing businesses are educated and trained. If we cannot mentor, model, and reinforce ethics and integrity in education, should we expect businesses to do so? The challenge is to find a way to both deter student cheating while also changing our educational institutions so that positive practices of academic integrity become so embedded that educational institutions will fall over themselves to protect them.

The Values Wars in Education

The business of education – money paid in exchange for "something else" – need not have created an environment ready for corruption. There are, after all, many businesses that are not corrupt, and money, goals, and success are not inherently immoral. Unfortunately, though, the trend toward valuing grades and degrees as ends in themselves has paralleled a trend away from values education and the responsibility of education to produce morally responsible citizens. In the war over the moral role of education, some fight for an education that is value-neutral while others fight for an education that instills values and shapes intellectually empowered moral citizens. These value wars, at their heart, are mostly about the search for a moral vocabulary for education that would either augment or replace older classical and religious themes that no longer seem applicable for a multicultural society. To be sure, part of the values wars was fought by those attempting to keep religious values central to education, but this fight usually remains on the periphery of the educational system, contained by the right of religious organizations to freely establish schools that teach their ascribed values. What is clear, however, is that citizens – whether religiously motivated or not – sense that something is missing in educating for citizenship. Neither "old time religion" nor "values clarification" by themselves has supplied a compelling moral vocabulary that can restrain even student cheating. "What to do about values" seems constantly contested.

Within our educational systems, there has been little discussion of what the substance of the curriculum should be and what values should be foundational to it. In the mid-twentieth century, two educational associations advocated for moral education and the teaching of "generally accepted values" such as "respect for the individual person, devotion to truth, commitment to brotherhood, and acceptance of

---

In the Opinion of Experts

Henry Giroux, notable critical theorist and proponent of education for democracy, has written about the influence of business on the de-emphasis of values in education. He writes, "it is not surprising that when matters of accountability become part of the language of school reform, they are divorced from broader considerations of ethics, equity, and justice. This type of corporate discourse . . . lacks a vision . . . [and] a self-critical inventory about its own ideology and its effects on society."

From "The corporate war against higher education," (2002, October). See www.henryagiroux.com

individual moral responsibility."[25] Despite these efforts, moral citizen education took a back seat to a focus on technical and academic subjects.

A late twentieth-century policy report from a prestigious private foundation noted "that higher education has become very adept at avoiding questions of purpose. Even discussions of the curriculum focused more on process than substance."[26] What has prevented this focus on substantive values education? Within a multicultural society, it is difficult to discover and establish which values are universal and should be embedded in public education and which are flexible and can be chosen as authoritative by a social group or culture. This phenomenon, otherwise known as cultural relativism, suggests that being a good citizen requires that one defers to the preferences of another group as long as some values are upheld as nearly absolute – such as condemning killing – and others as necessary for order – agreeing on which side of the road for drivers to proceed, for example – even if the decision is somewhat arbitrary.

Cultural relativism can account for some of the themes in the debates about academic honesty. Attitudes toward coaching/tutoring and attribution of sources may differ across cultures. But the problem of unauthorized collaboration – whether on a team project or homework – can be within cultures, also. Professors do have to clarify expectations and find ways to monitor and enforce them. If homework cannot be worked on jointly in an authorized way, how does the teacher: (1) clarify; (2) monitor; and (3) enforce? Failure to deliver on any one of these three can lead to widespread violation of the expectation and induce cynicism among students.

Process and substance could have been aligned if academic honesty had been identified as foundational to any curriculum. But it was not in the values wars debates. But why not? In part, it was because the language of academic honesty seemed reminiscent of older classical notions of the pursuit of truth. So, on one side of the debate, academic honesty and "truth" could be considered relative, difficult to define and even more difficult to inculcate or enforce. Even on the other side of the debate, to those devoted to the classical ideals of ancient Greek education, academic honesty was bypassed as a value that needed any attention or development. But why not among these traditionalists? There are several possible explanations, but one seems straightforward: student academic dishonesty was too mundane in the value wars when the very definition and fate of multiculturalism were the "hot" topics galvanizing "identity politics." Combine this with the crowded agenda of busing, sex education, school violence, and alcohol and drug abuse and one begins to realize why student cheating and academic honesty might not emerge as a central issue even though academic honesty is fundamental to the learning process.

Finding a Voice: The Movements against Cheating and toward Values Education

The movements to counter cheating in American education took shape in the early 1990s against this background of the commercialization of education and value wars. The character education movement became prominent in primary and secondary education arenas while the academic integrity movement has dominated the postsecondary education environment. The contemporary character education movement to counter student cheating was spirited by the Josephson Institute of Ethics when it brought together experts in ethics and character education to develop "a common language of core ethical values that transcend religious, political and socioeconomic differences."[27] This common language was termed the "Six Pillars of Character – trustworthiness, respect, responsibility, fairness, caring and citizenship." The CharacterCounts! initiative, born out of this meeting, helps elementary and secondary schools implement education that develops these character pillars and addresses student cheating.[28]

Around the same time, a parallel academic integrity movement was developing among postsecondary education faculty, students, and staff. In the early 1990s, a small group gathered together at a conference to discuss the perceived growth of student academic dishonesty and the Center for Academic Integrity (CAI) was born. A few years later, the Center developed their own moral vocabulary around "five fundamental values" – honesty, trust, fairness, respect, and responsibility. Now, the CAI is an international organization with a membership of over 480 high schools, colleges, and universities from several countries including Australia, Canada, Egypt, Greece, Grenada, Italy, Japan, Kuwait, Lebanon, Turkey, United Arab Emirates, and the United States.

An International Look

In 2005, the Australian government distributed *The National Framework for Values Education in Australian Schools*. This framework provides a vision for improving values education, eight Guiding Principles to support values education implementation, practice guidance, and nine values. The Australian nine values for values education mirror those endorsed by the Center for Academic Integrity and the Josephson Institute – care and compassion; doing your best; fairness; freedom; honesty and trustworthiness; integrity; respect; responsibility; and, understanding, tolerance and inclusion.

See www.valueseducation.edu.au for more information.

It is this consensus moral vocabulary, as illustrated in the parallel language of CAI and the Josephson Institute, which provided a partial truce in the value wars and supported attention to academic integrity. The CAI provided the somewhat clearer and more direct focus on the problem of student cheating, and its efforts have not only stimulated media interest but also changes in mission statements of schools to include values that directly support academic integrity. We now turn to the effort of the CAI to bring consensus to the debate on values, and we exhibit in detail how the five fundamental values are structured.

CAI "defines academic integrity as a commitment, even in the face of adversity, to five fundamental values: honesty, trust, fairness, respect, and responsibility."[29] *The Fundamental Values of Academic Integrity* publication of CAI in 1999 was important to the academic integrity movement because it established a positive vision for the movement rather than being preoccupied with revulsion at the epidemic of student cheating. It also helped the movement diversify its goals beyond diffusion of best practices to take into account how educational organizations can create stronger cultures of integrity. Page 4 of the document, for example, states:

> An academic community flourishes when its members are committed to the five fundamental values. Integrity is built upon continuous conversations about how these values are, or are not, embodied in institutional life. As these conversations connect with institutional mission statements and everyday policies and practices, a climate of integrity is sustained and nurtured.

The accessible moral vocabulary centers on integrity as a clustering of values beyond honesty. The ordering of the values as presented has a compelling logic and coherence. Honesty is presented first because the concern with student academic dishonesty initiated the academic integrity movement. But if dishonesty was the only concern, the movement would have been called "the academic honesty movement." Implicit in the academic integrity movement and CAI was the understanding that more was involved. By making explicit the four other values, *The Fundamental Values of Academic Integrity* authoritatively established that integrity is a *coherence* of values.

The second value articulated by the document was trust:

> People respond to consistent honesty with trust. . . . Only with trust can we believe in the research of others and move forward with new work. Only with trust can we collaborate with individuals, sharing information and ideas without fear that our work will be stolen, our careers stunted, or our reputations diminished. Only with trust can our communities believe in the social value and meaning of an institution's scholarship and degrees.

26

The third value is fairness, meaning "predictability, clear expectations, and a consistent and just response to dishonesty." Perceptions of fairness increase trust which, in turn, promote honesty. The fourth and fifth values, respect and responsibility, likewise contributed a sense of fairness and trust. But, like fairness, respect and responsibility require action and accountability. And the action was not to be a one-way street. Regarding respect, for example, teachers are expected to "show respect by taking students' ideas seriously, providing full and honest feedback on their work, valuing their aspirations and goals, and recognizing them as individuals."

With the fifth value, responsibility, we see the fullest expression of the need for "personal accountability and . . . action in the face of wrongdoing." This brings the discussion of integrity full circle given that action "even in the face of adversity" is a key to the very definition of academic integrity established at the beginning of the CAI document. But the most revealing of the challenges to building academic integrity is concealed by the document, that is, what to do about an obligation, implicit or explicit, for students to confront fellow students who cheat. Stating an obligation is one thing, but even the most successful honor-code schools with explicit rules for students to confront and turn in cheaters are often tortured by these "rat rules." The difficulty shown by the value of responsibility in this regard is perhaps the strongest challenge to building a strong academic integrity system on campuses. But no one said confronting academic dishonesty would be easy.

"Rat rules" provoke such soul-searching because whistle-blowing can incur personal and professional costs and fundamental values like loyalty inhibit people from exposing the failings of friends and colleagues (see the box on the following page). When one says "everyone does it," it is not only a rationalization of why one may cheat but also a guarded expression of "how do you really expect me to confront it?" The authors accept the conflict of values that can occur, yet firmly believe that a straightforward presentation of a problem of student academic dishonesty can lead to success for educational institutions and avoid the corrosive possibilities that cynicism or

---

In the News

"Teachers at [a high school in New York] voluntarily... accused administrators of changing... grades... [but the] cheating scandal... is still being kept under wraps... The worried teachers, who feel as though they have been left twisting in the wind... [were] allegedly told... that they will 'pay' ... with the loss of their pensions."

From *New York Teacher* (2007, December 6), "Wagner HS cheating scandal report delayed," by Jim Callaghan. Retrieved November 22, 2008, from www.uft.org/news

---

fatalism may instill if the issue of student academic dishonesty is not addressed.

The academic integrity movement is perhaps more needed now than ever before – not necessarily because more students are dishonest, but because there are more pressures on students, faculty, and administrators than ever before. Globalization, technology, competitiveness, and limited access to educational opportunities create an academic environment with competing interests, multiple vested constituencies, and conflicting values. The academic integrity movement is able to supply a common moral vocabulary that can provide a foundation upon which we can build cultures of integrity in schools, colleges, and universities.

Conclusion

The magnitude of the challenge of academic cheating is beyond what one or two small groups like the CAI or Josephson Institute can accomplish. The multidimensional and comprehensive efforts needed to confront student cheating must be broader and deeper. It is fundamentally a leadership challenge and will not be successfully addressed until *all* levels of education find leaders who can effectively respond to a growing public demand for action and accountability.

The business of education and the war over the values of education kept the discussion of academic cheating in the background but also shaped the emerging conversation about academic integrity. When news coverage of student cheating exploded in the 1970s and then surfaced again in the 1990s with real concerns of educational corruption, the conversations of business, culture, and academic integrity coalesced. "Values wars," ironically, made educational leaders more willing to use the concept of culture to understand their own organizations, and researchers began using the concept of culture to comprehend the student cheating problem.

For example, many researchers have stated that there is a culture of cheating on campuses[30] and that we are becoming "larger and more complex, losing the sense of shared culture, trust, and individual accountability."[31] This loss was partly due to the commercialization of education but also cultural relativism. The concept of culture thus became central in the discourse about what to do about cheating; "culture" reflects the persistence and deep-rooted qualities of cheating phenomena yet culture could also be seen as "civic," that is, as "a pluralistic culture based on communication and persuasion, a culture of consensus and diversity, a culture that permitted change but moderated it."[32] In the application of "culture," one can avoid pessimism about the prospects of confronting cheating while being realistic about the difficulty of doing so. Culture became a window into the essential mission of education.

The focus on the culture of cheating also renewed attention to values, and the challenge of articulating value-based instruction on campuses. The solution to the cheating problem became the reinvigoration of a culture of academic integrity, and the contemporary academic integrity movement was born. Attention to academic integrity enables a focus on values that does not fall apart in the face of many of the arguments stemming from the commercialization of education and from cultural relativism. The moral vocabulary of culture and values, although still a source of debate, became accessible to the mainstream of educators and provided an opportunity for those who found student academic dishonesty to be especially problematic to seek a new path to confront an old problem in our educational system.

So, from the distractions of the values wars and the business of education came new terms and ideas, accessible to the general public, that can move discourse beyond simple condemnations of student academic dishonesty and toward a more sophisticated approach which can be grasped not only by parents of elementary school students but by presidents of our most prestigious universities.

Overview of the Book

In this chapter we have seen why cheating is a "dark, deep secret" and how education has had some difficulty in addressing it. We also have seen the promise of the academic integrity movement and powerful, new ways to think about academic integrity. This effectively sets the stage for the remainder of this book which seeks to both define the problem and propose solutions that can be applied in all educational institutions, from elementary schools to postsecondary education. In Chapter 2, we further explore the nature of the student cheating problem by describing its historical and current state, as well as situating it within other concerns of corruption stemming from the dishonest acts of teachers, researchers, parents, and administrators. We argue that soon academic dishonesty and a failure to address it methodically will challenge the essential mission of education in terms of the teaching–learning environment, but the leverage associated with confronting student academic dishonesty will generate spillover effects into confronting other kinds of academic dishonesty and educational corruption.

Chapters 3 and 4 guide the reader from the external atmosphere into the core of the student cheating phenomenon by describing the ways in which students cheat and the determinants of such behaviors. These chapters provide teachers and parents with an insider's view into the secret lives of their students and expose the problem as pervasive and deep.

After this firm establishment of student cheating as the deep, dark secret of education, we move to the possibilities and hope of resolution. In Chapter 5 we discuss the short-term deterrents that teachers and faculty can use within their own classrooms to create environments in which academic integrity is made easier and more profitable than academic misconduct by students. In acknowledgement that teachers alone cannot change the cheating culture in our schools and colleges, Chapter 6 outlines the long-term deterrents that must be considered by campus faculty and administrators. Moral development and the institutionalization of academic integrity may be the most promising approaches to resolving the student cheating problem in the long term.

Chapter 7 is a call for action and wisdom in confronting student cheating. Here we accelerate our use of sample conversations that can stimulate students, teachers, administrators, and others to new levels of awareness that make inaction an unlikely option in dealing with student academic dishonesty. Too often, student academic dishonesty has been seen through only one window – the possible conversations as "teachable moments" when a teacher confronts a student cheater. Conversations are not just a beginning point in prompting moral and social action but are key to linking all educational stakeholders in the construction and maintenance of educational institutions of integrity.

Chapter 8 then further refines the tactics and strategies in dealing with the problem of student academic dishonesty, and Chapter 9 concludes with some provocative thoughts on finding the good in student cheating.

Chapter 2

The Nature and Prevalence of Student Cheating

"The more we focus on all the clever ways youngsters cheat, the more likely we are to ignore the fact that the biggest single factor in escalating academic dishonesty is the failure of parents and teachers to diligently teach, enforce, advocate, and model personal integrity."[1]

In the last chapter we established that student cheating is problematic because it can corrode the character of the individual student and, if it is systemic and widespread, it can corrode the integrity of the educational institution as a whole.

So, the question we will consider here is: what is the nature of the problem? Is it systemic and widespread, that is, an epidemic brought on by the failures of parents and teachers (and other school officials) to teach, enforce, advocate, and model personal integrity? Or, is it a simple matter of some kids "behaving badly," no matter the circumstances and educational environment?

Answering these questions is critical as they inform and focus our concerns, attention, and actions. If the problem of student cheating is simply an individual character issue, we can focus our attention locally at the micro level – the individual student, the small student group, the family unit, or perhaps most broadly on the classroom. We can introduce incentives to individual students for behaving well and implement punishment when those students behave poorly. If it is epidemic, however, our attention has to be global, at the macro level – the school-as-a-whole, the educational system, and society. At that point, we would have to move beyond the remediation of individual cheaters to a transformation of the factors within the educational system that encourage and support cheating and therefore discourage academic integrity.

Many argue that student cheating has reached an epidemic state, which is defined as a state in which something is "extremely prevalent or widespread" and perhaps even rapidly spreading or increasing in occurrence.[2] Donald McCabe of Rutgers University has been a particularly loud and effective voice proclaiming the epidemic problem of student cheating. According to McCabe, who has surveyed 80,000 students and 12,000 faculty in the United States and Canada between 2002 and 2005 (as well as thousands more students in the 1990s and in other countries), "cheating on tests and exams among undergraduate students is problematic on US and Canadian campuses, as roughly one in ten students admit to one or more instances of copying, using crib notes and/or helping someone else to cheat on a test or exam."[3] McCabe's data has provided fodder for much of the popular press outcry over the epidemic of student cheating. Take a look at just some of the headlines from the early twenty-first century:

- "Everyone does it: Academic cheating is at an all-time high. Can anything be done to stop it?"[4]
- "Students armed with technology usher in a new school of cheating."[5]
- "With more than half of Canadian university students cheating, all degrees are tainted. It's a national scandal. Why aren't schools doing more about it?"[6]
- "According to recent studies, academic dishonesty is rampant, with increasing numbers of students admitting to cheating"[7]

- "Cheating is on the rise: Surveys show less integrity among high school and college students."[8]
- "Varsity survey reveals that 49% of Cambridge students have committed some form of plagiaristic act whilst at the University."[9]

In this chapter, we explore the historical and current state of student cheating to establish a better understanding of the extent of the problem. Before we do that, we caution the reader to temper their interpretations of the figures we present. Because the majority of the data on student cheating is derived from students' self-reports of their own behaviors, we really only know what students *claim* to be doing, rather than what they *are actually* doing. In addition, most of the data only tell us what students say they have done "at least once in the past year." So, even if 100% of students admit to having cheated on a test once, for example, can we really claim anything about the extent of the problem reaching an epidemic state? We would argue that though these statistics present a rather incomplete picture, they can be used to illuminate a perspective on the extent of the problem because it is reasonable to suspect that students are underreporting, not overreporting, their behaviors. Why is this a reasonable assumption? First, self-report bias is known to occur in surveys that ask about socially taboo topics, so we can assume that if students admit to engaging in a behavior once, they have probably engaged in it more than once. And, second, the same survey studies demonstrate that faculty observe cheating on a much higher basis than students report engaging in it.[10] We turn now to a brief history of student cheating so that we might put the current state in a historical context. Is cheating a new problem? Is it worse than ever before?

A Brief History of Student Cheating

In *Academic Integrity in the Twenty-First Century: A Teaching and Learning Imperative*, one of this book's authors, Tricia Bertram

Gallant, offers an overview of the history of academic misconduct in the American college or university from the eighteenth through the twenty-first century.[11] This review illustrates that, at the very least, student cheating may be endemic, if not epidemic, to the educational system as a whole. In other words, student cheating certainly should not be seen as a recent phenomenon and should be understood as intimately linked to the characteristics, functions, and purposes of education. Personal characteristics of students have always played a part in shaping cheating behavior, but so too have situational factors (that is, nonproctored exams, teaching style of the professor, classroom environment, and chances of success), characteristics of the campus and educational system (that is, organizational moral climate, the pressure for grades, a lack of perceived connection between morality and academic misconduct), and fears of failure.

An International Look

The origin of academic cheating can perhaps be traced back to the origin of the standardized test movement which began in ancient China. At that time, "the Imperial examinations elevated cheating to . . . an art form in China. Miniature books [could] be concealed in [one's] palm; [parts of] the Confucian Classics [were] sewn inside [shirts;] . . . veteran scholars [were hired as exam proxies and] . . . examiners [were bribed] . . . These cheating methods, refined over centuries, are alive and well today."

From *China in Focus Magazine* (2002), "A unique experiment," by Justin Crozier. Retrieved November 21, 2008, from http://sacu.org/examinations.html

---

In the eighteenth century, for example, students who were at risk for failing their classes and the ensuing public humiliation of that failure would cheat in order to "save face" in the eyes of their peers. Cheating, then, was a way to maintain one's sense of personal honor because deceiving the teacher was more admirable than failing the class. When students were caught for cheating, they were normally expelled from the school, but even this removal did not end their academic cheating. Diploma mills became quite prevalent in America in the eighteenth century, and so students who had been expelled for cheating could easily secure a diploma and misrepresent their educational achievements for the purposes of securing employment. The importance of an educational credential for social mobility, then, has been relevant for much of educational history, not just in America but in many countries around the world.

In nineteenth-century America, and into the beginning of the twentieth century, postsecondary campuses substantially increased in size and students began to view courses and assignments as hurdles that had to be cleared in order to make personal and professional progress.[12] As many as 40 percent of surveyed students admitted to engaging in academic cheating during this time[13] and student cheating was cited as a major blight on the integrity of educational institutions:

> Nothing is more significant of the maladjustment existing in our universities than the frequency of dishonesty in connection with academic work. Many young men and women who are scrupulously honorable in other relationships of life seem to have little hesitancy in submitting themes and theses which they have not written, in bringing prepared "cribs" to examinations, and in conveying information to one another during the course of an examination. There is a not uncommon feeling that a state of war exists between faculty members and students – no mere game, where the canons of sportsmanship prevail, but a downright, ruthless struggle in which any method of overcoming the foe is justified. Their attitude can be partly explained by the unsympathetic attitude of some professors, and partly by the rather mechanical organization involving grades, warnings, and probation; but, certainly, the principal cause must be found in the failure of undergraduates to appreciate the value to themselves of serious and conscientious intellectual effort and achievement.[14]

The most interesting angle of the above quote from Angell is that it was written in 1928, yet could be read as relevant to our educational system and society today. Complaints of the "mechanical organization" of education, the strained relations between teachers and students, and the inability of students to appreciate the value of "intellectual effort and achievement" can be heard uttered by critics of education in the twenty-first century and, we are sure, will probably continue to be uttered for as long as the formal educational system exists!

By the middle of the twentieth century, postsecondary institutions had dramatically expanded and diversified. Some argued that this dramatic change in American colleges and universities, along with the turbulence of the Vietnam and Watergate era, led to an increase in student cheating.[15] The rise of term paper mills facilitated student cheating on written assignments, and the exposing of such resources led faculty across the country to report multiple students for plagiarism. Because postsecondary education became increasingly important to American society during this era, the public also became more interested in on-campus happenings. As a result, popular press reports of student cheating exploded in the middle of last century, lending an air of "crisis" to the situation and resulting in a demand for action on the part of colleges and universities.

William Bowers, while a doctoral student, surveyed 5,422 students at 99 American colleges and universities between 1962 and 1963 and found that as many as 56% of students admitted to plagiarism and 44% admitted to cheating on tests in some way.[16] In 1966, Shaffer, citing the Bowers study in addition to others, wrote that "evidence continues to accumulate that cheating is both prevalent and widely tolerated in American education. Numerous student surveys and occasional cheating scandals support a popular impression that student honesty is at a low level. Perhaps most disturbing are indications that cheating is becoming an ingrained part of student life in the United States."[17]

By the latter half of the twentieth century, it seemed well known that many American students were cheating throughout their educational career. Fred Schab, Professor Emeritus of the University of Georgia, surveyed over 4,000 high school students between 1969 and 1989 and found increasing rates of self-reported cheating and acceptance of cheating over that time frame.[18] For example:

- the students who admitted to using a cheat sheet during a test increased from 34% (1969) to 68% (1989);[19]
- copying another student's work increased from 58% (1969) to 93% (1979) to 98% (1989); and,
- use of others' words or ideas without citation, that is, plagiarism, increased from 67% (1969) to 76% (1989).

A 1980s' study of over 1,000 sixth-graders and 2,000 eleventh-graders in California found similar participation rates to Schab, but in this study the increase in rates was between grades, rather than over the years:

- while only 39% of sixth graders admitted to cheating on tests, 74% of eleventh-graders did; and,
- 41% of sixth graders admitted to plagiarism, versus 50% of eleventh-graders.[20]

The increase in cheating from lower grades to higher grades may be most simply explained by "Campbell's Law" which loosely translated says "the higher the stakes, the more likely people are to cheat."[21] And, as students progress in the educational system, the stakes become higher – graduation from high school is the minimum requirement for surviving in the twenty-first century economy, while the bachelor's degree is becoming mandatory. Being admitted into selective universities, securing financial aid, garnering "full-ride" scholarships, and earning admission into graduate and professor schools can all be seen as high stakes for students and parents in a world where education is the key to social mobility.

In the area of undergraduate cheating in the 1980s and 1990s, Donald McCabe, a professor at Rutgers University and co-founder of the Center for Academic Integrity, published the first multi-campus study since Bowers's mid-century study, finding that:

- 52% of undergraduates claimed to have cheated on a test at least once in the year previous;
- 54% of undergraduates admitted to plagiarism at least once in the year previous; and
- 49% admitted to collaborating on assignments meant to be independently completed.[22]

While rates of plagiarism had stayed virtually unchanged since Bower's study in the 1960s, the rates of test cheating and "unauthorized collaboration" had increased substantially.

Summary

This review of popular press and scholarly reports of the history of student cheating suggests that cheating is a perennial phenomenon in education, one that survives the annual reconfiguration of the student populations. Student cheating has always occurred, but perhaps the opportunities for cheating (thanks to technology), the numbers of students cheating, and the ways in which students cheat have expanded. To be sure, the definition of "student cheating" has expanded since the eighteenth century to include behaviors beyond examination cheating to plagiarism and unauthorized collaboration, which is a term that did not even appear until the latter half of the twentieth century.[23] (The way in which student cheating has changed will be further explored later in the chapter). The popular press coverage of student cheating may also have expanded over the years, leading folks to believe that student cheating has become a bigger problem than ever before. However, at the very least, the history of student cheating, as endemic to the educational system, conveys that the problem cannot be reduced down to a simple concern with some students "behaving badly."

So we turn now to an exploration of the contemporary state of the problem – how much cheating is occurring in the twenty-first century and what can we learn from examining the studies that have been conducted?

Extent of Student Cheating in the Early Twenty-First Century

In this section, we explore the recent research on the frequency of student cheating, including international statistics where available. First we review the research on secondary school students, and then move on to the undergraduate population, providing a comparison between the two where possible.

Secondary School Students

The Josephson Institute of Ethics is perhaps the most consistent source of information on student cheating in American high schools in the twenty-first century. The institute surveys thousands of students every two years. In 2004, of 24,763 students surveyed in 85 US secondary schools about their behaviors in the previous year, they found that:

- almost 62% admitted to cheating on examinations at least once, while 38% admitted to cheating two or more times;
- 35% admitted to plagiarism at least once while 18% admitted they had plagiarized two or more times; and,
- 83% admitted to copying homework from another student once in the year previous, while 64% admitted to doing it two or more times.[24]

When the Institute surveyed students again two years later in 2006, the percentages remained virtually unchanged, although almost 11,000 additional high school students (for a total of 35,000) completed the survey.[25] In 2008, only 30,000 students completed the survey (a drop from two years prior), but the figures have increased slightly from the 2004 levels.[26]

What may be important in the results of Michael Josephson's surveys is that a significantly higher percentage of students admit to academic cheating than other forms of dishonesty or misconduct (such as stealing or cheating in sports). This discrepancy may suggest one of two things: students are cheating more in school than in their personal lives, or students are more willing to admit their school cheating than other cheating behaviors. Either way, the higher self-reports of academic cheating imply that high school students perceive academic cheating to be more acceptable, or at least less morally disagreeable, than other forms of cheating or stealing.

Additional statistics from the Josephson survey lend credence to the hypothesis that students attach little social or moral stigma to academic cheating. In all three years, a majority of students (74–77%) indicated that they considered themselves to be more ethical than their peers, and almost all believed that honesty, ethics, and good character are very important qualities to possess (93% in 2008). It could be that the students do not see the majority of their behaviors as "cheating" or "unethical" and therefore do not equate their academic behaviors with being dishonest. Alternatively, Michael Josephson explains that the lack of consistency between student rhetoric and actions is a result of cynicism of the "real world"; approximately two-thirds of surveyed students in both years agreed that "success-ful people do what they have to do to win, even if others consider it cheating."[27]

Students, however, seem unable to accurately gauge their poten-tial for success; cheating is not the bailiwick of students who are at risk of failing and, thus, not being successful in school. According to Barbara Pytel, an education consultant and writer, high-achieving students, including those in Advanced Placement[28] classes in high school, "cheat on a regular basis."[29] So, despite the likelihood of these students being successful in academia, they are cheating anyway. Why would that be? In the first chapter, we implied that this is largely because of the focus on grades as the ends and the lack of values education to counterbalance this focus. However, more specific causes of academic misconduct are elaborated on in Chapter 3. At this point it is critical to understand that the "epidemic" of cheating is defined by the high rates of academic cheating, the willingness to admit to academic cheating, and the diversity of students who do cheat. The behaviors are not restricted to individual students or particular student groups, but are exhibited by most students across any artificial way we may have of dividing them.

College Students

We know much more about academic cheating at the college level because more research has been conducted with this population. Most of the data that is of use for the purposes of our discussion stems from the data collected by Donald McCabe of Rutgers University who has surveyed over a 100,000 students since 1990. The contemporary state of academic cheating by students is gleaned particularly from McCabe's data from over 80,000 American and Canadian students between 2002 and 2005.[30] According to McCabe, 21% of undergraduates admit to cheating in examinations (i.e., copying, using crib notes and/or helping someone else to cheat) at least once in a year period, while only 5% admit to using an electronic/digital device to cheat during an exam. Only 10% of graduate students admit to copying, using crib notes or helping someone else to cheat on examinations at least once during a year period, and only 2% admit to using an electronic/digital device. A much higher percentage of students (33% of undergraduates and 17% of graduate students) admit to having obtained knowledge of the test prior to taking it.

With respect to academic misconduct on written assignments, a larger percentage of undergraduates self-report engagement in plagiarism in McCabe's surveys; as few as 25%, and as many as 50%, admit to plagiarizing and fabricating/falsifying a bibliography. A smaller percentage, 8%, admitted to copying another person's work once during a year period. These statistics hold true with survey research conducted in other countries as well. For example, in 2008, the Cambridge University student newspaper, *Varsity*, surveyed over 1,000 students and found that 37% admit to using someone else's ideas without acknowledgement, while only 7% admitted to copying another person's work.[31]

Summarizing the rates of student academic misconduct in countries outside the United States and Canada is much more difficult given the paucity of published studies, particularly at the secondary or graduate school level. However, there have been studies conducted and Table 2.1 indicates the percentage of surveyed students who have reported engaging in three behaviors (exam cheating, plagiarism, or homework copying) at least once.

The research included in Table 2.1 does suggest that the rates of college student cheating (or the willingness to admit to cheating) do differ among countries. Why might this be? It could be that students' attitudes toward, and beliefs about, cheating are shaped by their cultural backgrounds, educational experiences, and national-social factors.[32] Robert Lupton, a professor of business in Central Washington University, and Kenneth Chapman, a business professor with California State University (Chico), for example, found that Russian and American business students differ in their beliefs about cheating. Specifically, "Russian students were more likely than the American students to believe that most students cheat on exams and out-of-class assignments, that cheating on one exam is not so bad and that it is OK to tell someone in a later section about an exam just completed."[33] The research findings of Maria Fátima Rocha and Aurora Teixeira, professors with the Universidade do Porto in Portugal, who surveyed over 7,000 students in 21 countries, support the hypothesis that rates and beliefs about cheating differ by country. In essence, they found that students in countries known to be the least corrupt have the lowest propensity to cheat (or admit to cheating).[34] Whether students cheat more or admit more readily to cheating is really insignificant; a willingness to report cheating indicates that students do not perceive of academic cheating as a morally reprehensible behavior.

Table 2.1 A comparison of cheating rates by country

	Australia[1]	China[2]	Finland[3]	Portugal[4]	Russia[5]	UK[6]	US/ Canada[7]
Exam cheating	22%	83%	14%	62%	70.2%	0%	21%
Plagiarism	38%	N/A	31%	N/A	62.1%	0%	50%
Homework copying	40%	N/A	22%	N/A	84.3%	8%	8%

[1] Brimble, Mark & Stevenson-Clarke, Peta, 2005, "Perceptions of the prevalence and seriousness of academic dishonesty in Australian universities," *The Australian Educational Researcher*, 32(3): 1–44.

[2] *The Epoch Times*, 2005, September 8, "83% of college students in China cheat on exams." Retrieved November 26, 2008 from http://english.epochtimes.com/news/5-9-8/32106.html. This article reports on a *China Youth Study* which randomly sampled 892 college students and found that "82.74 percent had cheated on exams. 8.86 percent have 'helped' their classmates to cheat on the exams. 80.66 percent are students whose academic performance rankings are medium or high."

[3] Björklund, Mikaela & Wenestam, Claes-Göran, 1999, "Academic cheating: Frequency, methods and causes." Retrieved May 1, 2008 from www.leeds.ac.uk/educol/documents/00001364.htm

[4] Fatima Rocha, Maria & Teixeira, Aurora, A. C., 2005, "College cheating in Portugal: Results from a large scale survey," FEP Working Papers, Research-Work in Progress-n. 197. The authors of this study surveyed students in economics and management courses in all ten Portuguese public universities, resulting in 2,675 valid survey responses.

[5] Poltorak, Yulia, 1995, "Cheating behavior among students of four Moscow institutions," *Higher Education*, 3(2): 225–46. This author surveyed 248 students from four Moscow postsecondary institutions.

[6] Franklyn-Stokes, Arlene & Newstead, Stephen, E., 1995, "Undergraduate cheating: Who does what and why?" *Studies in Higher Education*, 20(20): 159–72.

[7] McCabe, Donald L., 2005, "Cheating among college and university students: A North American perspective," *International Journal of Educational Integrity*, 1(1): 1–11 (p. 5).

Comparing Rates of Cheating by Education Levels

McCabe parses out cheating behaviors much more finely than does the Josephson Institute, so it is difficult to compare the statistics; however, Table 2.2 attempts to do just that. As can be seen from this table, though cheating on examinations and homework decreases from high school to college and from college to graduate school, plagiarism increases in college and then drops off again in graduate school. The increase in plagiarism from high school to college is likely a result of increased opportunities; undergraduates are more likely to be assigned complex writing projects than are high school students.

However, why in general might undergraduates report less cheating than high school students, and graduate students less cheating than undergraduates? If Campbell's Law held, we should see the self-reported rates of cheating increase as the stakes for the students become more pronounced. It is important to remind ourselves here that higher stakes in education include higher stakes in getting caught cheating; as students progress in their educational careers, the self-report bias may increase as students increasingly see the cheating behaviors as undesirable by the academy. It could also be that as students mature, they have also developed morally and ethically, and so they actually do engage less in cheating behaviors than they did as younger students. The reasoning is difficult to ascertain for certain, though, so we are left now to rely on speculation and assumptions. What may be the most important lesson here is: the earlier we attend to student cheating, the more relevant values education may be.

Table 2.2 A comparison of cheating rates by educational level

	High school	Undergraduate	Graduate student
Exam cheating	62%	21%	10%
Plagiarism	33%	50%	25%
Homework copying	83%	8%	4%

So If Cheating has Always Existed, Why does It Require Attention Now?

So it seems that student cheating has always existed, is endemic to the educational institution itself, and exists in colleges and universities around the world (albeit to different extents). In other words, student cheating in school is not earth-shattering news. However, given the rise in self-reported engagement in cheating over the years, it is conceivable that students' beliefs have shifted from viewing academic cheating as morally reprehensible to merely morally disagreeable. When people engage in behaviors characterized as morally reprehensible, they tend to do so in covert ways, hiding their engagement from others, especially those in authoritative positions (e.g., parents, teachers). And, when asked about the behaviors on surveys, they tend to underreport their engagement in those behaviors. It follows, then, that when people engage in behaviors characterized as merely morally disagreeable, they will be less concerned with being "found out" – they will engage in the behaviors more readily and more openly, and they will admit to their engagement more consistently when asked about it on surveys. Precautions may be taken and discovery might be embarrassing, but the offender may not fear severe repercussions.

A most illustrative proof of this shift in attitudes toward cheating may be found on the internet. Students, in a seemingly flagrant display, seem willing to demonstrate and proliferate ways to cheat on youtube.com, a popular video-sharing website (A third party website, see http://lawgeek.typepad.com/lawgeek/2008/02/students-demo-t.html, has linked to several demonstrations of student cheating). McCabe's research also suggests that students may be less likely to see many behaviors as moderate or serious cheating, behaviors such as limited plagiarism (only 57% of surveyed students), unauthorized collaboration (only 32% of surveyed students), fabricating or falsifying lab data (only 19% of surveyed students), and turning in a paper or homework assignment copied from another student (only 11% of surveyed students).

In Popular Opinion

On the Public Broadcasting System's website, www.pbs.org/
itsmylife, over 24,000 kids have responded to the question
"Which best describes how you feel about cheating?" While over
51% chose "it's wrong, and it's never okay to do it," 34% chose
"it's okay as long as you don't get caught" and 13% chose "it's
wrong, but it's okay in emergencies."

So, it seems clear that contemporary students, whether studying
in China, Russia, the UK, or North America, view certain academic
behaviors such as exam cheating and homework copying as merely
disagreeable and are thus more willing to engage in these behaviors.
The question then is – what has changed to make academic cheating less morally reprehensible?

Though there have been many changes, we suggest two in particular
have been influential: the information explosion and the expanding use
of collaboration in the classroom. These two are particularly influential
because they alter the core of the educational system in which students interact – the teaching and learning environment. Other factors
are also at play, of course, in providing justifications for student cheating, such as the business of education which supplants the achievement of a degree for the accumulation of knowledge. We further discuss
these other factors as causes of academic misconduct in Chapter 4.
For now, we focus on the effects of technology and collaborative learning as they create new opportunities for cheating, confuse students'
understanding of legitimate academic work, and make it more difficult to determine when a student is cheating.

The information explosion has been technologically driven,
and the new technologies increase opportunities to cheat. Though
McCabe's research has not found that students admit to engaging in
test cheating with electronic devices (such as cell phones) more than
with "old fashioned" resources such as cheat sheets, it is obvious that

technology increases the ease of cheating in many different ways. Students can, of course, easily access any piece of information they wish to have via their cell phone, personal digital assistant (PDA), or computer, whether that information is coming from a friend, the internet, or a memory drive internal to the device in use. This information can be accessed in class for tests or outside of class for papers. Perhaps most recognizable is the ease of plagiarism in the digital age. Students can easily copy and paste information from the internet into their papers or download an entire paper for submission. Again, the information explosion or internet has not created new forms of cheating, but it has democratized cheating, making cheating resources accessible to all; no longer do students have to be a part of a sorority or fraternity to have access to term papers and old exams.

The New Media

For an interesting take on the way in which the internet and computer are changing our conceptions of knowledge and information, watch the video by anthropology professor Michael Wesch of Kansas State University, "Web 2.0 . . . The Machine is Us/ing Us" at www.youtube.com/watch?v=6gmP4nk0EOE.

The information explosion has also altered the cheating landscape by changing the way in which information and knowledge are viewed. Before the information explosion, there was a sense that knowledge was built vertically, that is, on the shoulders of others who were recognizable and could thus be given attribution. The explosion of information suggests a more horizontal sense of knowledge creation coming from a multiplicity of directions and sources. Take Wikipedia, the online encyclopedia, as an illustrative example. The content of Wikipedia is not developed by a few resident experts who are known contributors to the site, but rather it is developed *for all, by all*. This horizontal and invisible building of knowledge leads to the sense that the internet is a mutual brain into which we can all tap.[35] Add to this the fact that cross-disciplinary, interdisciplinary, and collaborative work is now becoming more valued for academics and students alike; the virtual internet is changing the actual daily work of teachers and students who are expected to work less independently and more collaboratively.

The New Media

Wikipedia is an example of the horizontal creation of knowledge. There is not one author or one lead author, but multiple collaborators who build across one another's ideas. There is vertical knowledge building as well, but the underlying premise is that no one owns the knowledge created on Wikipedia. And, if no one owns it, then, students might ask, why would it need to be cited?

If written knowledge is seen as collaboratively constructed,[36] then it seems reasonable that written communication would begin to take on the attributes of oral communication. Attribution of sources in oral communication is much looser than in writing. When Barack Obama in February of 2008 was alleged to have plagiarized speech lines from the Governor of Massachusetts, the charge had little traction – and not simply because the governor was the co-chair of the "Obama for President" campaign. Rules of attribution in oral storytelling and speeches are not as strict – people co-opt good lines routinely, speakers are not expected to cite every source or contributor to their speech (because people assume that speakers often do not write their own speeches), and the velocity of storytelling does not lend itself to citing all sources. The information explosion, then, has worked to make information and knowledge become more like public or communal property than private.[37] As copyright and patent protection has grown in importance, the rest of knowledge seems fairer game to be further distributed, paraphrased poorly, and "used up." Gresham's law as applied to currency (bad currency drives out good) now seems to apply to most of knowledge itself: why attribute sources when knowledge is proliferating and has a short shelf life?

The proliferation of cheating opportunities, the ease of cheating, and the multiplicity of sources from which to draw suggests that plagiarism and student cheating have entered a qualitatively different stage. Developing a new etiquette for attribution of sources from the Web seems like a giant and futile effort, even as style guides continue to try to do so.[38] It seems especially so when paired with the growth of peer collaborative learning, team projects, and small group discussions in today's classrooms that have been precipitated by a pedagogical trend to move the focus of the class and learning from the teacher to the student.[39] Access to the Web for students reinforces the notion that teachers do not have a monopoly on information or knowledge, and what information students access to complete their academic assignments is often out of teacher control. In such contexts, validating student initiative may become more important than controlling student behavior.

Thus, cheating and plagiarism begin to seem like outmoded concerns, or, at least, limited to enforcement in more controllable situations, such as standardized tests used for assessment. Students overwhelmingly believe that sharing homework or accessing resources to satisfactorily complete homework is not wrong, and teachers have great difficulty preventing it. Many parents are complicit in this, if not active participants, as they readily help their children complete their schoolwork. But, of course, it becomes difficult to regulate cheating even when it is limited to enforcement on standardized examinations. The profitability of cheating on standardized tests seems to increase with each year. The *New York Times* published a front-page article on March 5, 2008, entitled "Next Question: Can Students Be Paid to Excel?" about the growing movement to give students financial rewards – cash – for improved performance on standardized examinations.[40] In America, teachers, too, are getting bonuses for score improvements by their students. In other parts of the world, teachers and administrators make extra cash by selling standardized exam questions and answers to families desperate to have their children secure one of the limited, coveted spots in a national university.[41] Just as grade inflation had the ironical result of increasing tendencies to cheat, cash awards for improvement of scores were bound to increase incentives to cheat in the absence of increased enforcement of rules against cheating. Standardized testing companies have attempted to ratchet up anti-cheating enforcement. Just as technology can fuel an arms race, technology can fuel cheating trends.

In The News

"An undetermined number of students in China, Taiwan and South Korea were able to raise their [GRE] scores substantially last year on the verbal part of the most widely used entrance exam . . . by logging on to Web sites in those countries that post questions and answers memorized by previous test takers."

From *The New York Times* (2002, August 8). "Officials link foreign websites to cheating on graduate admission exams," by Jacques Steinberg. Retrieved November 24, 2008, from www.nytimes.com

---

Arms races do not always lead to wars, and the technology of cheating does not automatically lead to higher cheating. However, if enforcement is not robust, or if students come to believe that everyone is doing it – even if they are not – the tendency to cheat will increase. Technology did drive the information explosion and changes in how education was understood: attention to technology as an aid to intentional cheating is less problematic than the change to the horizontal sense of knowledge creation discussed above. Whereas cheating on an exam where rules and enforcement are clear, intentionality to cheat in the myriad areas of homework, collaborative learning in the classroom and using sources from the Web is more difficult to define and thus repress. Teachers have had to become far more explicit about what constitutes unauthorized collaboration on an exercise or project, even as they encourage collaboration among students. This "mixed message" is received as such by many students. It is certainly more complicated than the older rules on cheating and plagiarism and is indicative that the nature of the problem of student cheating has begun to shift – although the older issues of cheating and plagiarism continue.

Technology, the business of education, the reluctance to teach values and moral conventions, the perceived relativism of acceptable academic standards, inconsistent attention and enforcement and the information explosion transform the issue of student cheating from one of kids "behaving badly" to the edge of systemic corruption.

Reaching an Unacceptable Level of Corruption

How Much Student Cheating is "Acceptable?"

As the earlier historical review illustrated, cheating is a natural or endemic part of schooling. Because those involved in the process of education are human, there will always exist the necessity of dealing with individuals who choose to "cheat" the system by finding ways to get around the requirements or rules. Some may argue, in fact, that the purpose of schooling is not to rid the system of cheaters but to work with the students to correct their deviant, yet normal, juvenile behavior. In Chapter 7, we will elaborate on moral development as one of the options for long-term deterrents of student cheating. However, it is our assumption that the readers of this book are not only concerned with the individual cheater (or even the handful of regular cheaters) in our schools. Such individual cheating is, if not acceptable, tolerable given our ability to handle them with existing policies and procedures.

But at what amount does individual cheating "tip" to become un-acceptable or intolerable? In other words, what is the threshold level of acceptable corruption? Can we quantify it with a percentage of students? McCabe suggests that it is problematic even when only 10 percent of surveyed students admit to cheating on an exam at least once during the period of one year.[42]

We suggest that the "acceptable" level of corruption cannot be quant-itatively measured simply by counting the numbers of students who admit to engaging in certain behaviors, although the increase in the willingness to admit to cheating over the decades suggests that the scale is tipping toward corruption. In other words, corruption may be more effectively measured by assessing people's attitudes toward the acceptability or seriousness of the behaviors. That is, which behaviors are viewed as morally reprehensible and which are viewed as merely disagreeable? If behaviors are viewed as merely disagree-able or "not serious forms of cheating," then we can accept that the spread of behaviors will continue and eventually corrupt the educa-tional system. Also, if students are admitting to engaging in beha-viors they consider to be "serious cheating," then we should also be concerned. Finally, if faculty consider a behavior to be serious cheat-ing but they admit to not reporting or handling the same behavior, we may also be concerned about the possibilities of corruption.

To explore, then, the current level of corruption, we turn back to the research by McCabe. Table 2.3 lists the percentage of North American students who rank a behavior (e.g., copying during an exam) as moderate or serious cheating and the percentage who admit to engaging in that behavior at least once in the year previous.[43] The numbers are provided for both undergraduates and graduate students so we can see a comparison again of student attitudes at different levels of education. In Table 2.3, we generally see that graduate students tend to view all of the cheating behaviors more seriously than do undergraduates.

When the same figures from Table 2.3 are presented in graphical form (see Figure 2.1, p. 56), we can see that undergraduate and graduate students self-report less engagement in those behaviors they consider

Table 2.3 A comparison of perceptions of cheating between undergraduate and graduate students

	Undergraduates		Graduate students	
	Moderate/ serious cheating	Engagement	Moderate/ serious cheating	Engagement
Copying during an exam	91%	10%	95%	4%
Plagiarism – extensive	91%	7%	94%	4%
Using unauthorized aid during exam	90%	7%	93%	3%
Submitting a paper written by someone else	89%	3%	92%	2%
Copying/turning in another's work	87%	7%	92%	4%
Learning what is on a test ahead of time	64%	33%	79%	17%
Fabricating/ falsifying biblio	58%	14%	74%	7%
Using false excuse to delay test taking	58%	16%	67%	9%
Plagiarism – limited	56%	37%	68%	25%
Unauthorized collaboration	32%	42%	54%	26%

Note: The statistics in this table are all from McCabe's research: McCabe, Donald L., 2005, "Cheating among college and university students: A North American perspective," *International Journal of Educational Integrity*, 1(1): 1–11.

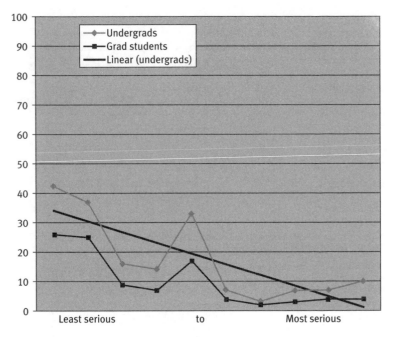

Figure 2.1   Statistics from Table 2.3, presented in graphical form

to be the most serious kinds of cheating behaviors. For example, undergraduate and graduate students are most likely to engage in "unauthorized collaboration" (the first point on the left of the figure), which is the behavior least likely to be considered moderate or serious cheating. On the other hand, the behavior considered by the majority of students to be serious cheating (copying during an exam), the tenth point on the graph, only 10% of undergraduates and 4% of graduate students admit to having engaged in this behavior at least once in a year period.

The graph also shows the expected pattern of decline in engagement in those behaviors ranked progressively more serious. This expected decline is only interrupted four times: at points 5, 8, 9, and 10, which represent "learning what's on a test ahead of time," "using unauthorized aid during exam," "extensive plagiarism," and "copying during an exam," respectively. Point 5 is particularly interesting – although over two-thirds of undergraduates and graduates rank this behavior as moderate or serious cheating, far more engage in it than they engage in some of the forms of cheating they consider less serious, such as using a false excuse.

What can we learn from this data? We suggest two important lessons: (1) an acceptable level of corruption may be being maintained; and, (2) the more experienced students are in education, the more seriously they view cheating.

Maintenance of an Acceptable Level of Corruption

To the first lesson – the statistics suggest that an acceptable level of corruption may be being maintained in our educational systems. Why do we say this? If you examine the statistics closely, you can see that, in most cases, the majority of surveyed students continue to consider the listed behaviors as moderate or serious forms of cheating (rather than trivial or not cheating). The only behavior for which this cor-relation does not hold true is "unauthorized collaboration" – only 32% of surveyed students see this as moderate or serious cheating (alternatively put, 67% see it as trivial or not cheating at all). This statistic is troublesome because, if unauthorized collaboration pro-liferates, it will compromise the validity of non-test assessments of individual ability (e.g., homework assignments). In other words, if homework and other non-test assignments are used to assess inde-pendent learning and ability, yet students rarely do these assignments by themselves, the ranking and evaluation system as we understand it can be corrupted.

Further evidence that we have thus far maintained an acceptable level of corruption can also be found in comparing student rates of engagement with the expected rates (given the students' rating of the seriousness of the behaviors). For example, if 68% of undergradu-ates consider unauthorized collaboration to be trivial or not cheat-ing as the research suggests, one would expect that an equal number of students would admit engaging in the behavior, yet only 42% do.

In other words, even though students may claim that a behavior is not serious cheating, their lack of willingness to engage (or admit to engaging) in the behavior suggests that they understand the behavior is unacceptable within the educational system.

However, having said that, there are three behaviors for which this claim does not hold true – copying during exams, learning what's on a test ahead of time, and limited plagiarism. In regard to these three behaviors, as many students admit to engaging in the behaviors as say that the behaviors are not-serious cheating. And, if students actually admit to engaging in behaviors they claim are trivial or not cheating, it adds some validity to their survey responses and suggests that they perceive little risk in admitting or engaging in the behaviors.

In general, however, the research can be used to successfully argue that students are self-monitoring their behavior according to their perceived seriousness of the behavior as cheating. Methods for controlling further corruption, then, should focus on reinforcing students' perceptions/definitions of cheating behaviors and perhaps influencing them to consider more behaviors to be serious cheating.

Student Development Leads to a Decrease in Cheating

Now to the second lesson we can glean from the research data. The difference in responses between undergraduates and graduates implies that the more experienced one is in education, the more one understands cheating behaviors. This could mean that cheating simply is a normal moral development or maturity issue – as students mature, they begin to develop stronger ethical compasses and adopt community standards. This interpretation is supported by McCabe's findings that younger students tend to justify even the most serious cheating with explanations of why they are not at fault.

An alternate explanation has to be considered, however, because these data points are not measures over time with the same population. Thus, the difference between undergraduate and graduate students could also mean that there is a generational difference, that the attitudes and behaviors of undergraduates reflect a new way of thinking about academic work, ways that are not held by those generations before them. We saw earlier that technology has altered the ways in which people think about information and knowledge, and the effect of the "net generation" on education is widely examined.[44] If the majority of students who admit to cheating "consider themselves to be morally responsible individuals," as some research suggests,[45] this may be cause for corruption concerns because it suggests that students' conception of the acceptability of cheating is tied less to their own internal ethical compasses and more to the situation or context in which they act.[46] And, if this is generational, these attitudes will carry through to graduate school and their professions. The research on student attitudes to cheating and their self-reported engagement in cheating, then, needs to continue to monitor students as they progress through educational levels.

Other Considerations

Currently, most education is still offered in a face-to-face environment, in the context of a relationship between a student and a teacher. Even in this environment, academic integrity is difficult to uphold and maintain (see the box on p. 60). Larry Hinman, an ethicist at the University of San Diego, reminds us that if we cannot establish environments of fairness, trust, honesty, responsibility, and respect in the context of the student–teacher relation, it is likely to be exponentially more difficult in "professor-less" courses – those conducted online or in packaged formats: "the incentive for being honest in these contexts must be primarily self-referential: without honesty, the student simply will not benefit from that particular educational experience."[47] The five fundamental values are "relational," Hinman notes.

Others,[48] however, suggest that such relational values can also be established in online environments, perhaps more so than in traditional face-to-face classrooms where there are hundreds of students for every one professor. In online environments, faculty can have a strong connection to students' work and the development of their

On Campus

The video "A Vision of Students Today" by Kansas State University anthropology professor, Michael Wesch, illustrates that even the face-to-face environment found in most public universities has profound effects on the way students engage in course work and relate to their professors. Students enrolled in an academic integrity seminar at one of the author's universities report that this video captures their experiences perfectly – they don't know their professors and their professors don't know them, so there is no relation upon which these fundamental values can be set. One student said, in a heart-wrenching tone, "I'm in my senior year and for the first time, I'm in a class where a professor knows my name."

(Source: www.youtube.com/watch?v=dGCJ46vyR9o)

skills, knowledge, and abilities because the "ongoing dialogue" between the student and instructor is retained in writing.[49] In addition, many online teachers are altering their pedagogical methods to be more student-centered, where there are fewer rote memorization assignments and more personal, interesting assignments on which students may be less likely to want to cheat.[50]

Student Cheating in the Midst of Greater Corruption

If the problem could be simply summarized as "students behaving badly," it actually might be fairly simple to address. We might start by clearly telling students what the rules are, punish their noncompliance, and reward them for compliance. We could train teachers and parents to use behavioral modification programs to help students improve their self-control to resist the immediate reinforcement that cheating achieves (that is, the completion of a difficult assignment). Unfortunately, the evidence we have found suggests that the problem of student cheating is not as simple as kids behaving badly. Rather, there is evidence that student cheating takes place in a corrupted system in which parents, teachers, and school administrators do not agree upon the rules, enforce rules, or demand academic integrity at all times. And, as mentioned earlier, student cheating seems to be directly connected with cheating and corruption, perceived or real, by adults. What is some of this evidence? Surveys conducted by Fred Schab, a psychology professor at the University of Georgia, for example, demonstrate that the percentage of parents who facilitate their child's engagement in academic misconduct may be increasing over time. In 1969, only 23% of high school students admitted that their parents had written a false excuse for them to get out of school or homework, but by 1989, 51% of parents had. It could be, of course, that there has been no increase in parental misconduct but that students simply feel more comfortable admitting their parental behaviors. Either way, this certainly does not seem like good news. Though most parents, if asked, could justify their false excuses, one does not have to think very deeply about the lessons that such behavior is teaching our next generation of parents.

Schab's surveys report some other disturbing trends:

- The number of students who believe that the majority of American people are honest has decreased from 49% in 1969 to 24% in 1989.
- Fewer students in 1989 (35%) than in 1969 (55%) believed that the majority of advertising is honest.

It is likely that if Schab's survey was repeated again in the twenty-first century, an even greater number of students may be shown to believe that the majority of adults are dishonest. There have been multiple, public examples of corruption in business (which led to the collapse of Enron and the housing and financial crises of 2008), religion (for example, the sex scandals revealed in the American Catholic Church in the early twenty-first century), as well as in politics (such as the indictment of Senator Ted Stevens of Alaska, also in 2008). Given that half of Alaska still voted for a convicted felon and the federal government bailed out the financial companies whose greed led to the financial crises – and all in a span of a couple of months in 2008 – it should not be surprising that our young students may see dishonesty and corruption as "merely disagreeable" rather than "morally reprehensible."

Three decades ago, Diana Amsden noted the connection between student cheating and educational corruption overall. Students cheat in an environment that allows ghostwritten papers, cheating on standardized tests, grade inflation, automatic grade level advancement, and parental aid on homework.[51] More recently, the International Institute for Educational Planning (of the United Nations Educational, Scientific and Cultural Organization) released two studies of educational corruption worldwide that demonstrate corruption by adults who serve as student mentors and teachers is proliferating.[52] Max Eckstein, writing for the International Institute for Educational Planning (IIEP) reports, for example, that educational staff in Britain, South Africa, and the United States have been known to help students cheat on standardized tests by either releasing the questions ahead of time, altering the results, or providing students with the answers. Postsecondary education faculty have been found to plagiarize others' material in their own publications, falsify their credentials, and fabricate research data.[53]

The diploma mill industry is flourishing around the world as adults choose to buy, rather than earn, credentials. The practice of acquiring fake certifications in order to receive pay raises or secure jobs is legal (or if illegal, unencumbered by legal or political supervision) in many states and countries. A 2002 news article published in the *International Herald Tribune*, a world edition of the *New York Times*, revealed startling information about the problem of fake credentials and standardized test cheating in China.[54] Ted Plafker, the article author, writes that some Chinese education officials suspect that as many as 500,000 people are holding fake diplomas (purchased for as little as $25 USD), a figure so staggering to China's Ministry of Education that a verification and accreditation system was established. That same year, the Educational Testing Service, which administers the Graduate Record Examination or GRE (the standardized test used by most American universities to admit students into masters or doctor of philosophy programs), suspended the computer science subject test in China because of the widespread practice of students posting test questions and answers to the internet.

In Popular Opinion

Adults do not set a very good example for our students when it comes to academic integrity. The most notable immoral exemplar may be found in the propensity of adults to buy educational certifications rather than earn them. The diploma mill industry is booming around the world, including in countries like the United States which prides itself on making higher education accessible and affordable to all people. Diploma mills are not illegal in every state or country, so the practice not only teaches students it is legal to fake an academic credential, but that it is a fairly widespread and acceptable practice. Why has this practice not been shut down by governments around the world? Some may blame the business of education – if there is a profit to be made, there will be someone ready to take it. Others claim that in shutting down diploma mills, you also hurt small unaccredited colleges.

For more information, simply type "diploma mills" in the search engine for *Inside Higher Education* or the *Chronicle of Higher Education*.

Academic misconduct around the world is not limited to students. Administrators in elementary through postsecondary institutions around the world have also been found to engage in behaviors that corrupt the educational system including plagiarizing another institution's documents, altering grades and student records, handing out unearned diplomas, falsifying enrollment numbers and financial records, and taking bribes to admit unqualified students.[55] Jacques Hallak and Muriel Poisson, also writing for IIEP, suggest that educational systems are vulnerable to such corruption because possession of an educational diploma has significant value in a knowledge society, the rules are often complex and implicit, there is usually poor regulation and oversight, teachers and administrators are poorly paid, and ethical norms are weak or unknown. Researchers are also not immune to the competition and pressures that lead students, teachers, and administrators to cheat (see the box on the next page for just one example of the many research misconduct stories available today). If students witness or even hear rumors of cheating by administrators, teachers, and researchers, how reasonable is it for us to expect that, amid all of this, students will have the courage and fortitude to resist engaging in the same types of behaviors?

In the News

"In August 2007, New York Attorney General Andrew Cuomo's probe into the student loan kickback scandal was expanded to assess evidence that universities had received perks from companies that operated their study-abroad programs."

From *Inside Higher Education* (2008, February 15). "Global U", by Andrew Ross. Retrieved February 15, 2008, from www.insidehighered.com

---

So, How Bad Is It?

Okay, you are wondering, I've seen all of the numbers, what does it all mean? Is student cheating in the twenty-first century a problem? Should I be worried about the corruption of individual character and the educational enterprise, or are the popular press and scholarly writers blowing this all out of proportion?

We, perhaps obviously, think you should be worried. Student cheating is endemic to the educational institution – it has always existed and it will always exist – and so we need to attend to it in order to keep it to an "acceptable" level of corruption. This is especially true now more than ever in the history of education because of the information explosion which increases the ease of cheating and alters conceptions of education, knowledge, and information. Teachers can help by educating young students on the five fundamental values of academic integrity (honesty, trust, responsibility, respect and fairness), by teaching basic academic standards such as citation and attribution, and by dealing with student cheating promptly and fairly when it is discovered. Parents can help by talking to their children about the valuing of learning and honesty over grades, by tempering their own desire for their children to succeed at all costs, and by supporting the teacher in disciplining their children when they are caught cheating. More on short- and long-term deterrents to cheating in Chapters 5 and 6.

But beyond being endemic to the educational institution, we believe the statistics demonstrate that student cheating is reaching an epidemic state, not necessarily because more students are cheating (although some surveys suggest that more are) but because the views of the behaviors seem to have changed from being "morally reprehensible" to "morally disagreeable" or even acceptable. And, research and practical experiences tell us that we may be tipping toward an unacceptable level of corruption because of the lack of willingness of students and faculty to call out the cheating behaviors they know to be going on. The obligation to report, common in traditional honor codes, has been modified in many schools because of students' reluctance to "rat" on their peers, and faculty routinely refuse to follow policy and report student cheating. For example, at the institution of one of the authors, only 2% of students are reported annually for cheating. Given the North American averages from McCabe's research, it is expected that as few as 3% and as many as 42% are cheating at least once a year. So, is an institution with a lower percentage of reported cheating uniquely honest? Doubtful; it is well known and admitted by faculty that the rate of cheating is much higher than what is reported. Thus, faculty and students allow cheating to continue in their classrooms and corrupt the teaching and learning process. We end this chapter with a conversation between a parent and a teacher that captures the nature of the problem. Then, in the next chapter, we focus more specifically on the techniques students use to cheat.

PARENT: You know, there was a lot of cheating going on when I was in school. It's not that big a deal.

TEACHER: I know, but students seem more brazen and rationalize it more easily now and, back in our day, parents stood beside the teacher in disciplining students who cheat.

Now the parents blame us and threaten lawsuits if we accuse their child of cheating.

PARENT: You are right. Students seem to think there is corruption everywhere – politics, business, professional sports, even in religions. And they're right! There *is* corruption everywhere – how are we supposed to counter that?

TEACHER: It's hard for students to grasp that we are trying to steer them away from that behavior, not train them for it! These are basically good kids – we just have to be clearer with them that cheating is unacceptable and explain why.

PARENT: Most parents are not going to help you do that – they are too concerned with Johnny getting into medical school and Suzie becoming a lawyer. The burden will be on you.

TEACHER: You bet – one more of many.

Okay, So It's Bad – Why?

In the next two chapters we continue to explore the extent and nature of the student cheating problem. So far, we've established that the problem is serious (it can lead to corruption of the individual student character and corruption of the educational system as a whole) and widespread (most students admit to doing it at least once a year and, given that they admit to doing it at all, the likelihood is that they are doing it even more often than that). So, the questions we now have to ask are – why do they do it and how do they do it? The reasons why they do it are varied – some are tied to the educational system problems we've already mentioned (the business of education, the lack of values education, and the rising influence of technology). Other reasons are situational and individual, and we'll explore the range of them. Then, we will drill more deeply into the "how" of student cheating in order to reveal what the students don't want their parents, teachers, and school administrators to know – the tricks of the trade. Once we have done that, we can move on to the second part of the book, which discusses the solutions to the student cheating problem.

Chapter 3

Reasons for Academic Dishonesty

Situation, Disposition, and Changing Times

"Cheating in high school is for grades. Cheating in college is for a career."

Anonymous student

We have seen that students have actively engaged in academic dishonesty from the beginnings of education to present times, and we've explored some differences in the extent of cheating between different levels of education and different countries. Now we turn our attention to the question "*why* do students cheat?" If you've just said, "that's easy, they cheat to get a better grade," you are absolutely correct. Getting a better grade is the overriding motive that drives academically dishonest behavior. However, research and student comments reveal a large number of specific issues that fuel the motive of getting a better grade. Several of these reasons reflect long-standing problems and obstacles that students traditionally confront, whereas other reasons are more recent in origin. Here are some of the more prevalent reasons and causes.

Situational Determinants

In the Opinion of Experts

"In a comprehensive set of studies done in the 1920s . . . psychologists . . . found [that] . . . virtually every child was willing to cheat under certain conditions . . . Some kids cheated on spelling tests, other kids cheated on math tests. Some kids cheated on Fridays, other kids only cheated when the teacher left the room."

From *Everybody Cheats*, a blog by Jonah Lehrer, an editor at large for *Seed Magazine*. See Jonah's blog, "The Frontal Cortex," at http://scienceblogs.com/cortex/2006/09/everybody_cheats_1.php

Often the situation(s) that students find themselves in are to blame, or are perceived as the cause, for the resulting academic dishonesty. Unfortunately, as modern society becomes increasingly complex and fast-paced, situational determinants, such as the ones we discuss below, are likely to assume an increasingly important role in academic misconduct.

Stress and Pressures

In 1941, psychologist Charles Drake conducted one of the earliest published pieces of research on cheating in the college classroom.[1] He reported that stresses and pressures for good grades were important determinants of cheating and concluded that "the crux of the situation is the competition for marks."[2] The results of a 1969 study, in which over 1,500 high school students were surveyed, indicated that fear of failure was the main reason the students gave for cheating; having to satisfy parental pressures and demands was the second most prevalent reason.[3] Perhaps personal experience can help you identify with the contention that students have perennially felt pressured by their parents to make good grades.

Other early researchers, such as the educator W. W. Ludeman,[4] suggested that when students perceived the course work as (a) meaningless, (b) overly difficult, or (c) overly easy, they were prompted to cheat. It is noteworthy that these pressures are mentioned by students in grade school, high school, and college. Several decades later, researchers find that students still cite pressures for good grades as a major reason for engaging in academic dishonesty.[5]

Why are good grades so important? Grades are one of the criteria that prospective employers and graduate schools use to select employees and graduate students, respectively. Low, or even average, grades may doom a student to not being hired or not being offered a position in a graduate program. Moreover, the emphasis that our society places on winning, whether it be in sports or business, is a factor that has increased the perceived importance of getting good grades (i.e., winning). We all want to be winners, whether it is in sports, business, or academics.[6]

Yes, grades can be directly related to a student's future. The quote that opened this chapter clearly reflects their importance. Here are some additional views from student respondents:[7]

- "I do study, but cheat to enhance my score."
- "I cheat so my GPA looks better to prospective employers."
- "Cheating is a way to stay competitive. I'll get As and have a good GPA and I'll have a good job or be able to get into a good grad school."

Certainly the stresses and pressures for good grades have not diminished during the past several decades. In fact, they may have become even more intense. Why? One reason is the increased number of students who are competing with each other. Although the increasing numbers may not be problematic in grade school, it definitely has become a factor by the time students reach high

---

In the Opinion of Experts

"Schools fail to reward, and in some way discourage, good behavior on the part of the students. When so much emphasis is placed on grades and individual achievement, the system seems to breed dishonesty. Students learn to succeed by all means possible, even if this means compromising their integrity to obtain high grades."

From Denise Pope's (2001) *"Doing School": How We are Creating a Generation of Stressed Out, Materialistic, and Miseducated Students* (p. 139), New Haven, CT: Yale University Press

---

school. At this educational level, students see grades as important for admission to a prestigious college. Thus, by the high school years the pressure to cheat is likely to escalate, even for the best and brightest students.[8] You should also keep in mind that many students mention the ease of cheating in high school as a factor that leads them to engage in academic dishonesty. This ease of cheating, combined with increased pressures for good grade point averages needed to secure college admission, may be more than many students can contend with; hence, they cheat. After all, they see everyone else doing it; why shouldn't they?

In their investigation of the reasons for cheating, psychologists at Midwestern State University in Wichita Falls, Texas found that many of the reasons that students gave for cheating fell into a category the researchers called *neutralization*.[9] Neutralization refers to the fact that students may attempt to justify their own cheating behaviors because of the similar actions of other students. For example, it is okay to cheat because "everyone else is doing it." Certainly, this logic does seem to fall into the *two wrongs can make a right* category.

The following conversation among several students uses several of these neutralizing justifications. As you read this conversation, keep in mind that these are all quotes from anonymous students who have reported cheating on exams:

STUDENT 1: A number of students around me left their papers uncovered. There was nothing to do but cheat. How about the rest of you?

STUDENT 2: The course material was too hard; I had to cheat.

STUDENT 3: The material in that course is meaningless; I'll never use it. So, why take the time and trouble to learn it?

STUDENT 4: I had to cheat because I'm in danger of losing my scholarship.

STUDENT 5: The instructor assigns too much material. I don't have time to learn it.

STUDENT 6: Remember when the instructor left the room during the test? He really doesn't care if I cheat.

STUDENT 7: One of my friends asked me to cheat; I couldn't say no.

STUDENT 8: The instructor really doesn't care if I learn this material.

STUDENT 9: I don't have enough time to study; I have to work to pay for my books and tuition.

Likewise, the number of students currently attending college has risen sharply in recent years and shows no signs of waning. More students mean larger classes and increased competition for good grades, and grades, as we just saw, are important keys to future employment or admission to graduate school.

In contemporary society, college students have to deal with additional stresses and pressures that did not confront students from earlier generations. Currently, the sons/daughters/members of affluent families are not the only persons enrolling in colleges and universities; today's students come from all economic levels. Consequently, finances may be a pressing issue for a large number of college students.[10] Yet, at the same time as enrollment has grown, there have been changes to financial aid programs that more intimately tie grades to a student's ability to get financial assistance;[11] these merit-based programs may add stress and pressure to students who would not be able to attend school without aid and, at that point, cheating may become a matter of survival.

Certainly, escalating costs for tuition and fees and textbooks have exacerbated this stress and will continue to do so for the foreseeable future. Although some students in previous decades may have had a part-time job, not everyone did; having a full-time job and being a student was unheard of. Currently, some type of employment while attending college may be the rule, rather than the exception. Moreover, this new norm appears to apply to both high school as well as college. With the costs of a college education continuing to escalate, this stress is likely to increase.

Add to this scenario the fact that the United States has become a much more consumer-oriented society during the past several decades and students' financial pressures mount even higher. Now, in addition to the costs of tuition, fees, textbooks, and room and board, students likely will have to add a monthly car payment, insurance premiums, and either monthly payments or credit card bills for such "necessities" as a big screen HD TV, cell phone service with all the options, premium cable or satellite TV service, and high speed internet access. Hence, many students do not see a job as a luxury but as a necessity. Because employment is mandated, there is less time for studying and educational pursuits assume a lower priority. The outcome should be clear; any options that save time and effort will be valued. Many students see cheating as one of these time-saving options:

- "I just don't have enough time to study."
- "My workload is too heavy."
- "Ten minutes of cheating is better than two hours of studying."

Other Situational Determinants

Research on academic dishonesty also has shown that many students willingly enter into collusion with other students to engage in cheating. In a nationwide study of cheating, one of the authors of this book, psychologist Stephen Davis, and his colleagues at Emporia State University (KS), found that many of the following reasons for this "collaboration" reflect the operation of various situational factors.[12]

74

In many instances it appears that some students may not plan to cheat until they arrive to take a test or the situation they find themselves in compels them to engage in academically dishonest behavior. Student explanations for cheating such as the following may fall under this category of being "compelled" to help another to cheat:

- He was bigger than me.
- I knew they needed to do good in order to pass the class. I felt sorry for them.
- I wouldn't want them to be mad at me.
- Because they might let me cheat off of them some time.
- No particular reason. It doesn't bother me because I probably have it wrong and so will they.
- I know they studied and knew the material, but test taking was really difficult.
- Just to do it. I didn't like the teacher, and I knew if I got caught nothing would happen.

Likely you read this list and, remembering the financial plight of many current college students, you are wondering about paying someone to give you "help" on a test. Surprisingly, only a small percentage of students engage in cheating on tests for cash. However, as you will see in the next chapter, students do not hesitate to pay others to complete their academic assignments – sales of reports and term papers are flourishing!

Several features of contemporary higher education also appear to have encouraged/facilitated academic dishonesty. For example, large, crowded classrooms foster cheating. With students sitting nearly on top of each other, it may be virtually impossible not to see the answer sheets of the students seated right around you. This situation is especially problematic because multiple-choice tests have become the standard testing format in many classes; most teachers simply do not have, or will not take, the time required to grade essay examinations. Hence, the answers to the tests question consist of single letters or numbers that are in plain sight and are easy to commit to

In the News

"Wal-Mart heiress Elizabeth Paige Laurie has surrendered her college degree following allegations that she cheated her way through [University of Southern California] . . . Laurie's roommate, Elena Martinez, [said] that she was paid $20,000 to write term papers and complete other assignments for the granddaughter of Wal-Mart co-founder."

From *The Union Tribune* (2005, October 20), "Wal-mart heir returns degree amid cheating claims," by Reuters. Retrieved November 24, 2008, from www.signonsandiego.com

memory, not paragraphs of written material that might be difficult to read and memorize. Certainly, if teachers carefully monitored the students during an exam, then crowding might not be such an important determinant of academic dishonesty. Of course, when many college classes enroll several hundred students, teachers will be quick to point out that they cannot monitor this large number of students by themselves; they need as much assistance as they can possibly receive. Even with the assistance of an army of proctors, the task is far from easy.

As discussed in earlier chapters, our contemporary society provides a strong motivation for students to engage in cheating in school. The attitude of "do it if you can get away with it" that society in general appears to hold serves to reinforce academic dishonesty. With society condoning such practices as using a radar detector to facilitate speeding on the highway, cheat sites to help one advance in computer gaming, and cheating on income tax payments, can approval (or at least acceptance) of academic dishonesty be far behind? Have situations like these helped create conditions where many students believe that cheating is a normal way of life? It would appear that the answer to this question is a resounding yes! Hardly a week goes by without there being a news story about some type of cheating scandal. Perhaps there is a message here for all of us! Are we setting especially good examples or being the type of role models that reinforce academic *honesty* for today's students.

Dispositional Determinants

At one time researchers may have entertained the possibility that there was a "cheating personality," a certain type of personality that predisposes a person to cheat. If this truly was the case, then psychologists could isolate individuals with this personality type and develop appropriate corrective measures. Unfortunately, this possibility has not fared well under the scrutiny of controlled research studies; there simply does not appear to be a single personality type that is unique to students who cheat.[13] On the other hand, personality research has identified several characteristics of students who engage in academic dishonesty. Although each and every one of these characteristics is not found in all academically dishonest students and do not paint the complete picture of cheating, they bring us closer to our understanding of why students may engage in this behavior. So, what are some of these elusive characteristics?

Male–female differences Let's begin with the obvious question: "who cheats more, men or women"? Although the results are inconsistent, generally speaking it appears that men are guilty of academic dishonesty more often than women.[14] However, before the women start cheering and the men start hunting us down to do us bodily harm, we hasten to add that the gender difference is not very large and has not been found in each and every research study.[15] In addition, much of cheating research depends on self-reports, so it could be that men are more willing to self-report cheating, and men dominate the fields where the greatest amount of cheating is reported (e.g., business, engineering). So, men may admit to cheating more readily, cheat more because they are men, or cheat more because they find themselves more often in "cheating cultures." The point is, we really do not know definitively if differences exist between genders and if they do, why.

Intelligence   One study in the seventies found that both high school and college students who have higher intelligence (as measured by an IQ test) cheat less often than students with lower intelligence.[16] Perhaps the course material is perceived as much more difficult by the lower-intelligence students and they feel compelled to cheat in order to receive a passing grade. However, we lack sufficient empirical research to make conclusive statements linking intelligence with cheating propensity.

Work ethic and moral development   Students with a high personal work ethic are less likely to cheat than are students with a low personal work ethic. In fact, research conducted by psychologists Eisenberg and Shank demonstrated that students with a high work ethic continued to work on a task much longer before they resorted to cheating than did students with a low work ethic.[17] Similarly, early research indicated that a person's level of moral development was negatively related to cheating; lower moral development levels were associated with higher levels of cheating.[18] However, more recent research has failed to replicate these early findings; hence, despite its intrinsic appeal, no firm conclusions can be made about the relation of cheating and moral development.[19]

Motivation   Motivation is another factor that may be linked to cheating. However, motivation is a rather large and unwieldy construct; hence, researchers have been forced to study specific aspects of this construct. Depending on the factor being studied, the findings have differed substantially. For example, several studies have investigated the relation between the time-urgent, competitive, in-control Type A individual and academic dishonesty. Because these individuals are very competitive, most researchers assumed that Type A students would show high levels of cheating; this has not been the case.[20] Under normal circumstances the percentage of

Type A students who cheat appears to be no different than the overall, general percentage of cheaters. Only in situations where control, such as being able to study or determine the correct answer, is taken away do we find that a significantly higher rate of cheating for Type A students.[21] In short, when Type A students perceive that they are not in control of their own destiny, then they are more likely than their more laid-back Type B counterparts to engage in academic dishonesty.

In the News

"A graduate of San Francisco's independent Urban School . . . now a junior at the University of Southern California, says, 'Everyone cheats . . . In college, there is no room for error. You cannot fail . . . so . . . that's why people resort to paying others to do their papers. Because you feel: Mess up once and you are screwed.'"

From *The San Francisco Chronicle* (2007, September 9), "Everybody does it," by Regan McMahon. Retrieved February 5, 2008, from www.sfgate.com

---

Whether students are motivated to learn the course material or whether they are motivated only by the lure of good grades is a good predictor of academic dishonesty. Students whose motivation is just for good grades are much more likely to cheat. In support of this contention, Matthew Huss, a forensic psychologist at Creighton University (Omaha, Nebraska), and his colleagues reported research showing that grade-oriented college students were more likely to cheat than students who were learning oriented. It is noteworthy that the motivation to obtain good grades is an external factor; research has shown that students who are externally (or extrinsically) motivated are more likely to cheat. For example, grade school children who expected a reward for high test scores were more likely to cheat than children who were less concerned with receiving a reward for high test performance. We will have much more to say about the importance of external factors throughout this chapter.

Need for approval   The need for approval also appears to be positively related to academic dishonesty; the higher their need for approval, the more likely people are to engage in academic dishonesty.[22] Because being very sociable or outgoing (extroverted) are often indicators of a need for approval, these characteristics also are predictors, but not especially strong ones, of cheating.

Student perceptions   How the students perceive the testing situation is another good predictor of academic dishonesty. For example, students who overestimate the amount of cheating, see students around them who do not cover their papers, and believe that a cheating opportunity presented itself because the instructor left the room are more likely to engage in cheating themselves. As we saw, these behaviors constitute the *neutralization effect*. Clearly, cheaters who hold these attitudes are refusing to take responsibility for their behavior.

Moreover, students who have a cynical attitude to cheating are more likely to cheat. Additionally, students who have a more tolerant, less condemning view of academic dishonesty are more likely to cheat.

Risk   As we have seen, students whose behavior is determined by external forces are more likely to cheat. Hence, the nature or fluctuation of such external forces should have an influence on the amount of cheating. It does. When externally motivated students perceive the situation as having lowered risk, academic dishonesty increases.[23]

Procrastination and responsibility   It likely will not be a big surprise for you to learn that students who are habitual procrastinators are more likely to engage in academic dishonesty. Procrastination is perhaps the most common reason or excuse students give when they reflect on their cheating during an academic integrity seminar at one of the authors' universities. Conversely, students who score more highly on a measure of responsibility are less likely to cheat.

On Campus

At one unnamed high-achievement campus (where the entering freshmen average GPA is above 4.0), pressure to succeed is the most commonly cited reason for cheating given by students who have been found in violation of the academic integrity policy. However, it doesn't take more than a cursory read of their personally written case studies to see that procrastination is a major factor. For all of the "pressures to succeed," students seem unable or unwilling to manage their time appropriately and put in the hard work necessary to succeed. So, when all else fails, they seem to make unethical choices in hopes of succeeding (that is, completing the assignment and securing a good grade) despite lack of effort and/or ability.

Changes in Attitudes, Values, and Morals

We believe that changes in students' attitudes, values, and morals are among the most powerful determinants of academic dishonesty. Now, we *do* understand that every generation of teachers loudly proclaims that "today's students just aren't like they were when I was in school." We all share these views and memories of the "good old days." We acknowledge that in some instances our comments may reflect nothing more than reminiscences and wishful thinking. In short, there may be no real differences between contemporary students and those of past generations. We hope this is true for a large percentage of today's students. On the other hand, we also believe that the values and attitudes of today's academically dishonest students may have changed substantially.

External Factors

We have mentioned that students whose lives are controlled by external forces are much more likely to cheat than students who have strong internal controls determining their course of action. Can we be a bit more specific and identify some of these external forces? Several factors that we have considered should quickly come to mind; among these factors are stresses and pressures, crowded classes, using multiple-choice tests, and so forth.

As students become controlled more and more by external forces, there is a corresponding decrease in internal control and conventional standards for ethics and morality. This line of reasoning brings us to another conclusion; because they lack or have lowered internal control, students who cheat most likely will not accept responsibility for their actions. They see the blame residing in the external forces that compelled them to cheat. The following comments from college students who are self-reported cheaters clearly reflect placing blame on external factors. Again we see neutralization at work.

- "The class was too hard."
- "Didn't like the teacher."
- "Had to work extra hours and couldn't study."
- "Don't like to see lazy students who cheat get better grades than me."

One student put this changing morality into bold relief by saying that "old morals and new times just don't mix."

Receiving an Education versus Receiving a Degree

The value that students place on receiving an education has diminished in recent years thanks in part to the growing business of education (which we discussed in the first chapter). Now, before you remind us of the large number of students who are currently attending colleges and receiving degrees, we want to make a clear distinction between receiving an education and receiving a degree. *Receiving a degree* means just that: the student receives a diploma, whether it is from high school, an undergraduate program, or a graduate program. Ideally, receiving a degree should depend on students demonstrating that they have successfully broadened their education. Unfortunately, these two activities are not necessarily connected to each other. For example, a substantial number of students start an educational program but do not complete it (i.e., do not receive a degree). These students may have received an education, or at least part of the prescribed educational experience, but not received the diploma. Even though they did not complete the degree program, their knowledge may have been expanded considerably. These students have benefited from their educational experience.

A more insidious situation occurs when the student receives the diploma without receiving the corresponding educational benefits and increase in knowledge. These students are not prepared to fit into society in the manner that their degree signifies. Unfortunately, more and more students, especially those who are hardcore, repeat cheaters, may fall into the category of students who value the diploma but not the education. Indeed, the majority of students today (75%, compared to 42% in 1966) value "being very well off financially" more than other educational values, such as "developing a philosophy of life."[24] The following conversation among some students will help put this devaluing of the educational experience in sharper focus. Because the views of Students 2 and 3 are actual comments from anonymous student respondents, the seriousness of this situation is even clearer.

STUDENT 1: We have seen a lot of cheating in our classes recently. How do you feel about this behavior?

STUDENT 2: I am aware of how much cheating goes on among my fellow students, and frankly, I am not surprised. It is not the experience itself that matters . . . it is the grades and the degree that you receive at the end that everyone cares about. College is a means to getting a career and an idealized style of life. And, in the view of many students, if cheating is the way to obtain the degree, so be it.

STUDENT 3: College is nothing more than a series of hurdles on the way to getting a good job. Any way you can get over the hurdles is all right.

Academic Dishonesty as a Victimless Crime

As we have seen, the shift in behavior control from an internal to an external focus results in students finding "excuses" (i.e., external causes) for their behavior. This view appears to have resulted in or coincided with a change in how a large number of academically dishonest students view cheating. Many of these students have told us that they view cheating as a victimless crime. Yes, the cheater may benefit from his or her dishonest activities, but these actions do not have an impact on anyone else. Hence, it is not wrong to cheat; no one is going to get hurt. Here are some student comments that reflect these sentiments.

- "Cheating is like adultery – what they don't know won't hurt them."
- "Cheating is no big deal; it's a victimless crime."
- "I don't feel guilty. I feel good because I'm going to get a good grade."
- "Cheating has become a guiltless type of thing."
- "If someone says that I can cheat off their paper, it's not wrong."
- "I know it's wrong to cheat, but it's wronger [sic] for me to get an F."

A New View of Academic Ownership

Recent years have also witnessed a changing view of academic ownership. Consider, for example, the following scenario. You are a student who has just purchased a term paper from either the internet or from an enterprising person who specializes in ghostwriting term papers. (The number of such ghostwriters who sell papers to college students is a mushrooming business.) You, in turn, present the paper you just purchased to your instructor to satisfy a course requirement. Most students from previous generations likely would see this behavior as an incident of academic dishonesty. On the other hand, numerous contemporary students see nothing wrong with this conduct. Because they purchased the paper, it was *their* property; therefore, they were turning in *their* paper when they presented it to the instructor. Clearly, at least in their eyes, they were not cheating. The views of many students are aptly summarized by one student who indicated that

"Since I bought the paper, it is my work."

On Campus

We saw in an earlier box that wealthy students are willing to pay others to do their academic assignments for them, and that, as college and university become more expensive, more students with the ability but the lack of funds may feel forced to do so as a matter of economic survival. The problem, however, is not restricted to single exchanges between two individuals – the term paper business is big business. Nick Mamatas, an author, confesses to his previous line of work as a term paper writer while in college in an article titled "The term paper artist: The lucrative industry behind higher ed's failings."

"Writing model term papers is above-board and perfectly legal . . . indulgent parents even buy papers for children too young for credit cards of their own . . . Perhaps unsurprisingly, the plurality of clients was business administration majors, but both elementary education majors and would-be social workers showed up aplenty."

For more on this story, read the article online at http://www.thesmartset.com/article/article10100801.aspx.

Figure 3.1 summarizes the multitude of factors that can influence whether a student engages in academic dishonesty.

It is likely that change in attitudes and values was one of the precipitating factors that prompted the Liberty Mutual company to initiate the Responsibility Project. In this regard, it should not surprise you that, as the number of cheaters continues to escalate, the amount of responsibility shown in our society decreases. The Responsibility Project was developed to provide an open forum for people to express their views on responsibility. According to Liberty Mutual: "We believe that the more people think and talk about responsibility, and even debate what it means, the more it can affect how we live our daily lives. And perhaps, in this small way, together, we can make the world just a little better."[25] We encourage you to explore the Responsibility Project website (www.responsibilityproject.org) and take part in this stimulating project.

In summary, we believe that there has been a change in the attitudes, values, and morals of students who engage in academic dishonesty. This is a different generation, many of whom have accepted cheating (or redefined behaviors formally seen as cheating as acceptable) as a way of getting through school. Unfortunately, the attitudes of the students who do *not* engage in academic dishonesty may have *contributed* to the widespread nature of this behavior. It would

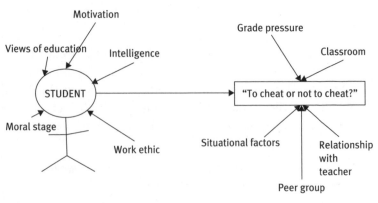

Figure 3.1 Determinants of student cheating

86

appear that the noncheaters are well aware of the extent of cheating. However, the great majority of these students do or say nothing about the cheating they observe. These behaviors probably give cheaters the impression that the noncheaters condone this behavior. What the noncheaters seem to have forgotten is that if cheating results in higher grades for the academically dishonest students, then this behavior definitely can alter the relative standing of the students in a class. In short, academic dishonesty is *not* a victimless crime where no one is hurt – grade point and class standing are important criteria that admissions committees use to determine college admissions and the distribution of scholarships.

We close this chapter with the following, sobering comment from an anonymous self-reported cheater. Think about it!

"Apologize for what? I would do it again!"

Chapter 4

From Cheat Sheet to Text Messaging

The Evolution of Techniques

"Sit against the wall when you cheat. Fewer people will see you and rat you out; and the teacher comes by less often."

Anonymous student

Academic dishonesty has been, and continues to be, an enduring problem in contemporary society. In this chapter we'll look at how students are cheating across all grade levels. Despite the wide variety of techniques, you will see that some behaviors remain consistent across all age groups and academic levels. The following conversation between two parents will set the stage for our discussion of cheating techniques.

PARENT 1: When I was in high school I saw an appreciable number of my classmates cheat on tests, book reports, lab reports, and term papers. You name it and someone was trying to find a way to get a better grade without having to work for it.

PARENT 2: Yes, I also saw the same behaviors. Although some of my classmates came up with some pretty clever ways to cheat, these schemes always seemed to fall into one of two

89

categories: looking on someone else's paper or taking some sort of cheat sheet to use during the test. Did the behaviors you saw fall into these two categories?

PARENT 1: I agree, those were the most popular behaviors I saw in high school. Things were a little different when I got to college. For example, I often saw one student taking an exam in the place of another student. One of my friends was a psychology major and he frequently took psychology exams for his friends who were not doing well in their introductory psychology classes. Of course, this scheme only worked in very large classes of several hundred students where the teacher did not know the students' names or faces. How about you, did you encounter any unusual cheating practices?

PARENT 2: The one that stands out in my mind is the development of signals where one student signals the number of a question and then indicates which answer is correct. However, this scheme only worked with multiple-choice and true–false questions; however, there were always a large number of those questions on each test.

Grade School

Although there is scant information on academic dishonesty among grade school children, it appears that looking on someone else's paper during a test is a likely candidate for "most popular technique." Other popular techniques appear to include copying other students' assignments, plagiarism, and having parents completely prepare assignments.

One of the most insidious forms of cheating associated with the primary grades to emerge in recent years involves cheating on competency or achievement tests, such as the Texas Assessment of Knowledge and Skills (TAKS) test.[1] Such cheating appears to be occurring in two distinct ways. First, the curriculum is purposely structured so that only those topics that are directly related to the

On Campus

For a wonderful book about cheating that can be used to teach grade school students about cheating, pick up *Cheater Pants* by Barbara Park. The story teaches students about the difference between cheating and collaboration and establishes cheating as morally reprehensible, albeit it in a funny, nonthreatening, way.

achievement tests are presented to the students. Why should we consider this practice to be an example of academic dishonesty? Because it purposely may deprive the students of an appropriate, broad-based education, we believe it belongs in this category. In this example, though, the teachers or curriculum specialists, not the students, control the curriculum; and therefore they should assume the blame.

A second dishonest practice involves students copying answers or teachers and administrators giving the students the tests or correct answers before the administration date. Clearly, this behavior is a blatant example of academic dishonesty. How prevalent is this behavior? An article in the June 4, 2007, issue of the *Tyler Morning Telegraph* (TX) reported that: "In a story published in its Sunday edition, *The Dallas Morning News* said it reviewed statewide scores from 2005 and 2006 on the Texas Assessment of Knowledge and Skills test, which is given in grades three through 11."[2] The newspaper said it found evidence of cheating by more than 50,000 students, who either copied answers from others or had their answer sheets doctored by school staff.

Similar newspaper articles from other parts of the country indicate that this is a widespread phenomenon. Such scandals have sent state education officials scurrying to try to implement more effect test security measures. For example, in response to the problem of cheating on the TAKS, Texas Education Association officials proposed a new security plan. A June 12, 2007, Associated Press release indicated that: "The plan includes assigning test monitors to campuses with previous security problems, using multiple versions of tests and mandatory seating charts at test sites. A bill waiting approval by Gov. Rick Perry, meanwhile, would replace the state's high-stakes high school exit exam with end-of-course tests."[3]

High School

As you just saw, by the time students reach high school, academic dishonesty is a favorite activity for a disappointingly large number of students. In fact, academic dishonesty appears to peak in high school. The techniques that were popular in the lower grades continue to be popular. However, some new techniques begin to make their appearance. For example, although test cheating techniques still include the ever-popular looking on a classmate's paper, it has been joined by making crib notes/cheat sheets, writing the answers on a desk, using a system of pre-arranged signals to communicate answers, and obtaining copies of the test before the exam period. If these procedures sound outdated to you, you may be overestimating student use of technology or more sophisticated cheating methods. Consider the following incident that occurred in Hanover, NH in 2007. Two groups of students broke into the Hanover High School just before the end-of-the-term final exams were scheduled to be administered. Some students acted as sentries while other students used stolen keys to enter teachers' filing cabinets and steal exams for several courses. Authorities estimated that a total of 50 students were involved.[4]

As another example that incorporates old and new cheating methods, school officials in Chapel Hill, NC caught a group of students in February of 2008 who had a master key to the Chapel Hill High School in their possession. The group, which it appears numbered as many as 30 students, used the key to enter offices to steal tests or photograph exam answers by using their camera phones. Though the audacity of student behaviors that jump the line between unethical and criminal behavior may be sufficiently

---

On Campus

Test anxiety and stress may only increase for middle school students in the twenty-first century. "The College Board . . . unveiled a new test for middle-school students to provide . . . information on . . . student [sic] readiness for college. But critics say this test is unnecessary . . . [because] there is already a pre-SAT and the SAT test . . . [and] students are tested every year in third through eighth grade because of . . . No Child Left Behind."

From *Diverse* (2008, October 22), "College board unveils controversial new test for middle-school students," by Robin Chen Delos. Retrieved October 22, 2008, from www.diverseeducation.com

---

shocking, what is even more amazing is that this master key had been passed from one student group to the next over several years.[5] We might ask ourselves how many other groups of students managed the same feat without being caught?

Not all of the cheating in high school is this outrageous or adventurist. Plagiarism, whether it is copying from classmates or other sources, such as encyclopedias, continues to be prevalent. Additionally, high school is the time when students begin changing (or simply fabricating) data on laboratory reports in their chemistry, biology, or physics classes especially.

College

The variety of techniques, as well as the diversity of venues, really mushrooms and reaches a zenith when we evaluate academic dishonesty at the collegiate level. Also, our examination of cheating in college requires that we examine different settings/opportunities that include classroom tests, laboratory reports, internet plagiarism, and online classes. Let's consider each of these different venues.

Classroom Tests

Comments from over 21,000 anonymous student respondents have revealed an almost unbelievable diversity of ways that students have cheated on classroom examinations.[6] The methods used to cheat on classroom tests appear to fall into three classes: using unauthorized materials, helping/being helped, and using technology.

Using unauthorized materials is exactly what the designation implies – the student has access to and uses materials that the instructor has prohibited in order to more accurately answer test questions. For example, earlier we told you two stories of students who gained entrance into high schools to secure copies of tests ahead of testing time; although such stories are often attributed to urban legend or historical oddities, gaining illegal entrance to a school to steal copies of tests is definitely still alive and well as a technique that students use to engage in academic dishonesty, whether in high school or college. These techniques are not restricted to accessing tests. At one university we know of, students gained access to the area in which end-of-semester grades were being stored before they were submitted to the registrar's office; the students erased their assigned final grades on the Scantrons for several courses so they could "award" themselves the A grades they wish they had earned honestly.

As we saw in the earlier conversation between two parents, using a cheat sheet is perhaps one of the two most popular and oldest techniques for cheating on classroom tests. However, this technique has come a long way since the schooldays of today's parents! The following modifications that students have devised should convince you that some students have taken the use of unauthorized aid to new levels of creativity and deviousness.[7] Anticipating the comment you are likely going to make when you finish reading about these techniques, we definitely agree: if only we could harness all of this creative energy and channel it in a more academically productive direction! Consider the following:

- "I hid a calculator down my pants." A clever arrangement that leaves you wondering how the calculator was retrieved and used during the test.
- "The answers were tape recorded before the test and I just took my Walkman to class and listened to the answers during the test."
- Numerous students have reported taking the label off bottled water (e.g., Evian) and writing the answers on the back of the label and replacing it on the plastic bottle. These students are quick to caution that the bottle should not be opened because the water helps magnify the answers.

On Campus

The water bottle technique seems old – fashioned when you consider how students use scanners and computers to remake the actual label to store examination information. Just type "coke bottle cheating" in the YouTube search engine and you will find several demonstrations intended to aid students in this cheating technique.

- Many cheaters have written answers on Band-Aids, bandages, and even on casts on their arms or legs.
- As the following quotes indicate, writing answers on body parts also is a favorite technique. "I've done everything from writing all the way up my arm to having notes in a plastic bag inside my mouth." "I wrote the answers on my thigh and just raised my skirt to see them during the test."
- Answers also can (and have) been written on the visor of a ball cap, shoe soles, tissue, or on the inside of reflective

---

On Campus

A student at one university we know of was observed looking often at both of her shoes during an exam, so the professor asked to see her soles and, sure enough, crib notes covered the bottom of her shoes! A picture of the soles served as sufficient evidence for that case when it went in front of a hearing board.

---

sunglasses. One inventive student said, "I would make a paper flower, write notes on it, and then pin it on my blouse."

- Several students indicated that they took two blue books to an essay exam. They completed one of the blue books at home prior to the exam. The second blue book was placed in the common pile of blank bluebooks. At the completion of the exam, the student turns in the already completed blue book and takes home the blank one he or she received at the beginning of the test.

- Schools that still use older Scantron machines to electronically score multiple-choice tests may have a problem they are unaware of. Several cheaters report that they have cheated in the following manner. First they mark an answer for each question in pencil. Then they use lip balm to mark all the remaining answers for each question. Because the machine reads the lip balm as a marked answer, the student receives a perfect score in the test because all have been marked. The instructor, who doesn't see the lip balm, doesn't check the answers.

- "I had a copy of the test and looked up the answers ahead of time and memorized them."

- "I opened up my book [during the test] and looked up the answers."

On Campus

Student use of old exams is getting easier, again with technology. Postyourtest.com, for example, allows students to upload and download exams and answer keys for free; in fact, the company has even paid students in Starbucks gift cards for uploading the material. No longer do students have to belong to fraternities or sororities to access test files!

Helping/being helped also has yielded some creative, collaborative methods to engage in academic dishonesty. Consider these five techniques shared by undergraduates:

- A substantial contingent of cheaters reported developing a code that they and one of more classmates shared. "We worked out a system of hand and feet positions." Other students indicated that each corner of the desk top represented an answer for a multiple-choice question; one student would signal a question number and the partner would simply touch a corner of the desk top to signify the answer.
- One student purposely drops the answer sheet; a cohort picks up the dropped sheet.
- One student fills in two Scantron answer sheets and passes the second sheet to the accomplice.
- Writing the answers on a large eraser and then sharing the eraser with a friend.
- Large classes having several hundred anonymous students have encouraged another academically dishonest practice: trading places. In this technique, a student who is not registered for a particular class takes the place of a registered student during an examination. The unauthorized student typically is a major in the subject being tested or has already taken the test in question.

The Evolution of Techniques

As the following examples of cheating on tests indicate, students have been quick to make use of *technological advances* to assist them in academically dishonest pursuits.

- Student respondents report that the popularity of programmable calculators skyrocketed when they discovered that these devices could send messages (such as answers to test questions) from one calculator to another.
- Several, apparently more affluent, students have used the miniature camera-pager technique. In this procedure, one student takes a miniature camera into the testing situation. The camera may be worn as part of a piece of jewelry (women) or part of a fraternity pin (men), and so forth. The student uses the camera to send a picture of the test to an outside accomplice. The accomplice looks up the answers to the test questions and sends them via an alpha-numeric pager to the student taking the test.
- When the Graduate Record Exam (GRE) was given in a paper-and-pencil format on the same day across the country, several enterprising cheaters secured copies of the exam early in the morning on the East Coast. Then they prepared a cheat sheet with the correct answers and flew the cheat sheet and a paying client to the West Coast where the client took and aced the GRE. In these cases, time-zone differences combined with improved air travel provided a hard-to-detect cheating technique.
- Students also have made effective use of miniature computers to aid their academically dishonest pursuits. For example, a substantial number of cheaters report that they have taped a Palm Pilot computer to their leg before taking an exam. Because they wore baggy shorts to the exam, all they had to do to access the computer (i.e., test answers) was to raise a leg of their shorts.
- Currently, the most blatant use of technology involves the use of cell phones. Text-messaging provides students with an easy way they can share answers during a test.

In the News

Students are not the only ones who share answers to standardized tests – businesses are born out of this insatiable desire for high scores. "Scoretop.com . . . published. . . . 'live' questions on its . . . GMAT preparation [web]site. It charged prospective MBA students $30 a month to have access to its VIP service. Those that took them up on the offer were then encouraged to memorise GMAT questions themselves so that they could be posted on the site."

From *Financial Times* (2008, July 9), "GMAT and FBI expose test cheats," by Della Bradshaw & Sara Mishkin. Retrieved November 24, 2008, from www.ft.com

The New Media

ChaCha is the newest text messaging service that can assist students who maybe do not have friends or classmates who will help them during a test. At www.chacha.com, they describe the service as "like having a smart friend you can call or text for answers on your cell phone anytime for free! ChaCha . . . allows people with any mobile phone device . . . to ask any question in conversational English and receive an accurate answer as a text message in just a few minutes."

If students do not cheat during a test, they can still try afterwards. One popular method for cheating in universities with large classes is "altering a graded exam for re-grade." This technique takes advantage of the good graces of the teaching assistant or instructor who acknowledge that they sometimes make errors in grading and therefore allow students to resubmit graded exams if such an error is discovered. Students will change their incorrect answers and then resubmit the exam claiming that the grader made an error; if the teaching assistant or instructor does not have a copy of the originally submitted exam, it can be difficult to detect this dishonesty – and students know it.

Laboratory Reports

Many college students report that they do not see anything wrong with changing (or completely fabricating) the data for a laboratory report. For example, one researcher found that over 80% of the students she sampled had modified laboratory data and did not believe that their behavior was wrong if it suited their needs. The following conversation between two students illustrates this view.

STUDENT 1: Why don't you actually gather and turn in the lab data in the manner prescribed by the instructor?

STUDENT 2: The data that you collect and turn in isn't important. What is important is the experience of preparing the laboratory report in the correct format and I'm receiving the full benefit of that experience.

Although this behavior may not seem especially egregious, the long-term implications are more sobering. Consider the (very real) possibility that some of the students who changed or completely fabricated data on their college laboratory reports may complete graduate training and become research scientists. It is highly likely that their research will be supported by federal grants at some point in their careers. What will keep them from modifying/fabricating their grant-supported research data if the results of their projects do not turn out as they predicted in their grant proposals? Nothing. We know of several instances where this type of behavior has occurred.

Fabricating or falsifying lab data is just one technique for cheating on laboratory reports. Many more students routinely copy previously submitted lab reports or copy the answers/data generated by others and claim it as their own work. This allows the student to not even attempt the lab. Although, again, students do not see this copying as cheating, it is as equally troubling as fabricating data. Students who do this not only fake their accomplishment of specific lab techniques, but fail to learn the skill of communicating scientific findings. One might not worry if students were taking these courses as electives, but most often those who do this are majoring in science and plan on becoming doctors or researchers. We wonder what kind of world we'll be living in if such students reach their professional goals?

Internet Plagiarism

Although today's students continue to plagiarize from printed sources and the work of other students as did previous generations, the internet offers a new and apparently very appealing venue for securing term papers and reports. If you haven't visited such a site, do a Google search for "term papers"; you will be amazed at the results. Our efforts were rewarded with 9,550,000 hits!

One of these sites (http://www.1millionpapers.com) had a very large number of papers that students could order. We entered the search term "academic dishonesty" and were offered over 200 papers to choose from. One titled "Academic Dishonesty" was described as "9 pages in length. Academic dishonesty, like all other forms of deviance, has important sociological dimensions . . . [so] it will be important to address such theories as strain theory, opportunity theory, differential association theory and labeling theory, all of which provide some type of motivation for this behavior. Bibliography contains 11 sources."[8] For only $9.99/page you receive a same-day download for your chosen paper and a free bibliography. Hence, the paper we just described would cost $89.55. This may seem a bit pricey, but for some students the saving in the time they would have to spend preparing such a paper from scratch is well worth the money.

On Campus

These sites point to a disturbing facet of the evolution of cheating techniques – those that cost money, such as buying a ghost-written paper, are less likely to be detected than those techniques that are free, such as copying a report from a previous student or copying and pasting material from online texts and websites. As a result, there is a very real likelihood that we primarily catch and punish the least advantaged (e.g., first generation, economically disadvantaged) of our college students, while enabling the privileged to cheat their way through college.

Another website that you will find interesting is www.chuckiii.com, which purports to be "dedicated to helping students with their everyday college needs." Certainly, the pages of this site that deal with such topics as "Do you know what plagiarism *really* is?" and "Do you know how to properly cite sources?" do have the potential to offer students some genuine assistance. On the other hand, the lure of 30,000 free term papers, essays and book reports is likely to be very tempting to students inclined to engage in academic dishonesty. Unfortunately, it would appear that many of these free papers were sent to this site by students. The site features an appeal for students to "keep them coming and help us grow." Of course, there are reports and papers for sale. Probably these for-sale papers are better written, more thoroughly researched, and have a more extensive bibliography. Additionally, there are numerous links to other, similar sites; obviously, distributing and selling papers is big business.

Online Classes

Clearly the internet offers students abundant opportunities for plagiarism. Unfortunately, plagiarism is not the only venue for academic dishonesty that the internet offers.

In recent years terms such as "distance learning" and "online classes" have become commonplace in higher education. The original approach taken by such courses was to have an on-campus teacher simultaneously instruct students at several satellite locations. Usually, this arrangement was accomplished via a telephone hookup and speaker phones so that students and teacher could talk to each other. Subsequent variations of this basic setup used television and allowed students and teacher to see and converse with each other. Certainly, adding a visual component was an advance over simple audio communication. However, students still had to travel to the satellite centers where the television facilities were located.

Then, the expanding capabilities of the internet changed everything. Now, *online classes* can be taught by a professor in Texas who has students taking the class in their homes in Michigan, Indiana, California, Wyoming, Ireland, Spain (literally anywhere the students have a computer and access to the internet). Currently it is possible to complete entire undergraduate and graduate courses and degrees online. Clearly, technology has helped bring college courses and degrees within the grasp of many more people and in a very user-friendly manner.

However, before you applaud these technological advances too much, you should be aware that online courses also are subject to academically dishonest practices. The most troublesome aspects involve testing and assignments.

Without question, is it difficult to envision how an instructor would administer an examination to students in an online class, especially if the students are located around the world. If tests are an integral component of the course and students take them online, then trouble can arise rather quickly. For example, it is difficult, if not impossible, for the instructor to know who actually answered the questions on the examinations. That concern has led many instructors to substitute assignments in place of tests in online classes. However, this solution does not fare much better than giving tests. In short, unlike the face-to-face classroom where teachers can actually see students write papers and become accustomed to individual abilities and writing styles, in an online class the teacher never knows who, the student or an accomplice, actually completes the assignments.

Beyond the Undergraduate Level

Unfortunately, cheating does not cease when students complete their undergraduate degrees. Most students will enter the workforce and find nonacademic ways to cheat in society in general (e.g., cheating on your income tax and the use of radar detectors to exceed the speed limit and avoid police radar traps are common examples). However, a sizeable number of students will continue their educational pursuits in graduate and professional programs. In these venues academic dishonesty, which continues unabated, takes on a whole new and perhaps more personal dimension. These are individuals who are now training to become accountants, lawyers, physicians, and so forth.

In the News

In an Indiana dentistry school, 9 students were dismissed for breaking into a computer to sneak a look at an upcoming exam, 16 were suspended for being involved in the incident, and 21 others were reprimanded for "violating [the school's] professional code of conduct by knowing about and not reporting the incident." The school felt strongly that the students had to be punished "because, [according to the Dean] it certifies that graduates 'can be trusted to do the absolute right thing in every situation in their professional lives, even when nobody is looking.'"

From *Inside Higher Education* (2007, May 10), "Cheating on a different level," by Elia Powers. Retrieved May 10, 2007, from www.insidehighered.com

---

And *you* will come in direct contact with them and use their "expertise" and "skills"! Just as the academically dishonest behavior makes the transition from the cheaters' undergraduate career to their graduate/professional school years, so do the preferred techniques; the use of unauthorized materials or looking at a neighbor's paper during a test, plagiarism on written assignments, and data fabrication abound.

Yes, students have devised numerous techniques to engage in academic dishonesty. Once again, we can only wish that students would direct the energies that they devote to academically dishonest behavior in more constructive directions. The following conversation suggests that students may not see any alternative:

STUDENT 1: Are you ready for the test tomorrow?

STUDENT 2: No, I've had to work extra hours this week and I haven't had any time to prepare. How about you?

STUDENT 1: I had to get a second part-time job in order to pay my rent; it just went up again.

STUDENT 2: Looks like I'm going to have to find some way to take the answers with me to the test in order to get the grade I need.

STUDENT 1: Me too.

This Sounds Bad – Is There Nothing We Can Do?

Before you begin to feel too distraught over the picture we have painted in these first four chapters, we invite you to pause and reflect on the reality of the situation. Yes, academic cheating is corrosive to the individual student's character and the integrity of the educational system as a whole. And yes, there are many factors that contribute to a student's propensity to cheat and thus it may be difficult to attend to all of them. And finally, yes, students have multiple methods for cheating and it can be overwhelming to think of preventing every method from coming to fruition. However, it is also true that:

1. Student cheating is not new to education, so we have proven methods to reduce opportunities and temptations for cheating;
2. If we can accept that cheating is a natural youth behavior, we can know that it is appropriate and right to respond to cheating when we do see it;
3. Students are young adults who most likely will mature out of a propensity for cheating if we can effectively guide them; and,
4. Not at students cheat all the time, and so there is the possibility of harnessing the honesty factor that is largely present on our campuses.

In the remaining five chapters of the book, we guide you through each of these possibilities for moving past despair and frustration to hope and action.

Chapter 5

Short-Term Deterrents

Strategies for Class, Labs, and Online Testing

_____

"Nothing short of dismemberment will stop me from cheating."

So far we've looked at academic dishonesty from several vantage points. We've raised such issues as how many students are involved, why they are cheating, and whether there been a change in values, attitudes, and morals. Now we turn our attention to a consideration of what can (and should) be done to stem the tide of what appears to be a tsunami-like wave of academic dishonesty. As you will see, combating academic dishonesty is a multifaceted and challenging issue.

Just mentioning the topic of preventing academic dishonesty raises a number of related questions such as:

1. What methods are available and being used to detect cheating?
2. What are the appropriate/inappropriate responses to academic dishonesty if it is detected?
3. What penalties have been or should be given for various types of academic dishonesty?

Let's look at each of these issues before we tackle our main topic of what to do to deter cheating, at least in the short run.

Detection

Tests

If you conducted a poll and asked the average person on the street how they would detect cheating on a test, they most likely would say "I would *see* it." Observation is one of the two primary methods for detecting cheating on a test.[1] Although observation is one of the most common forms of detecting cheating on tests, it comes loaded with problems. For example, during a test several students may pause and gaze around the room as they consider a question or ponder an answer; they may give the impression that they are cheating by looking at a neighbor's paper, but are they? Should you confront these students? You have no evidence, and unless they confess, you will never know for sure. On the other hand, if you *observe* a student using a cheat sheet or other unauthorized materials, you have evidence and a much stronger case.[2] Although directly observing cheating taking place is desirable, this approach gives the teacher very few options to choose from. For example, if the teacher is at the front of the classroom, then the likelihood of cheating on the part of students in the back of the room goes up. Hence, the teacher's best option is to circulate throughout the room during the test; vigilance should be the operative word.

Here's an all-too-familiar scenario that will introduce the second main method for detecting cheating on tests.

TEACHER 1:	I just finished grading the exam I gave yesterday. Two students turned in papers with *exactly* the same answers, both correct and incorrect.
TEACHER 2:	Did they sit close to each other?
TEACHER 1:	Yes, and they are best friends.
TEACHER 2:	I think I would look into this matter a bit further.

How should Teacher 1 deal with this situation? Did these two students cheat? Because they sat close to each other, the instructor might be very tempted to say "yes." If you accuse the students of cheating, how certain can you be of your accusation? Some teachers attempt to strengthen their case for academic dishonesty in situations like these by using a statistical procedure to determine the chance or probability that these two (or more) papers would have identical answers. The smaller the probability (i.e., the less likely the chances of the answers being the same), the stronger the case that cheating was involved. However, because nothing is ever proven absolutely, there always will be that little bit of doubt. This just might be that one time in two million that the students under suspicion did not cheat; their papers were identical just by chance. Also, if the students in question are best friends, it also is quite possible that they studied together and learned essentially the same correct and incorrect material. When viewed in this manner, it seems to appear that cheating may not have been involved.

On Campus

Teachers and faculty should know that most school policies do not require you to prove cheating before reporting it – the process that initiates as a result of reporting suspected cheating can work that out.

These concerns notwithstanding, recent advances in computer technology have prompted the development of computer software to detect cheating. This is a large and growing market; for example, a recent Google search for "software to detect cheating on tests" yielded 273,000 hits. One of these vendors, Assessment Systems Corporation (assess.com/xcart/home.php) offers a variety of products, including "Scrutiny!" – one of the first programs to be developed. According to this website,

Scrutiny! is designed to:

- assess multiple-choice test center integrity by screening test center test results for instances of possible copying, either from other examinees or by using common answer sets provided by others; and
- compare the test results of examinees who have been accused of copying from other examinees on multiple-choice tests and true–false tests. Scrutiny! produces a report that estimates the probability that the responses of pairs of examinees to the test questions were arrived at independently.

Some classroom teachers are making use of such statistical programs to aid them in combating cheating on tests, but the method is much more commonly used by large, commercial testing companies. For example, the Educational Testing Service (ETS) uses a statistical procedure called the K-index to determine if the *incorrect* answers of two people taking one of their tests are unusually alike.[3]

Even though the statistical procedures are mathematically sophisticated and seem to be growing in popularity, they are far from perfect. For example, they only address the probability that one student copied from another student. Clearly, the statistical procedures are not designed to detect the use of unauthorized materials, such as cheat sheets and technology (e.g., text messaging). Moreover, for the current statistical methods to be effective, the cheating has to be rather extensive. In short, these methods do not detect cheating when two students copy only a few times on a test.[4] Clearly, these procedures need further refinement.

Plagiarism

For years faculty have detected plagiarism by comparing papers that students turned in. Such comparisons typically fall into one of two categories: (a) comparing papers turned in by students in the same class or in different sections of the same class, and (b) comparing student papers with already published books and journal articles. Before you start saying that no students would be dumb enough to turn in the same paper, let us assure you that often two or more students will submit the *same* paper, often to the *same* instructor! Personal experience supports this last statement. One of the authors of this book once received identical papers, including typos, from two students in the same class. When asked why they did this, they indicated that they thought they "could get away with it."

Noting that the writing style and quality of writing changes abruptly can also be a key to detecting the presence of possible plagiarism. Such abrupt changes may send teachers to the library or the internet to check the student's references for plagiarized passages. A comparison of a suspect paper with a sample of the student's other work in the course also may raise questions about plagiarism.

As computer technology has advanced, so has the detection of plagiarism. Currently an abundance of software exists for the detection of plagiarism. A recent Google search for "plagiarism detection" yielded 110,000 hits! Admittedly, a substantial number of these sites dealt with computer software plagiarism. However, a large number of the sites were concerned with academic plagiarism. For example, one of the most popular sites, Turnitin (turnitin.com), proclaims that: "Used by thousands of institutions in over eighty countries, Turnitin's comprehensive plagiarism prevention system lets you quickly and effectively check all of your students' work in a fraction of the time necessary to scan a few suspect papers using a search engine."

Of course, all of the products at Turnitin are available for a fee. The cost of subscribing to this service and the time required for the evaluation of a large number of papers has kept some colleges and universities from using these services. A teacher doesn't need sophisticated computer programs to detect plagiarism, though. Most often, plagiarism can be detected by googling key phrases in a student's paper that stand out as odd – either overly sophisticated sentences or those filled with facts that the student must have read from an outside source – but lack a citation. The reader only has to type the suspicious phrase in google.com or scholar.google.com with quotation marks, and you'll likely pull up the source copied by the student.

One other caveat about plagiarism detection systems – despite their appeal of ease and convenience, it is important to keep in mind that such software is not infallible. Some researchers and teachers argue that none of these computerized systems can provide conclusive evidence of plagiarism, and in fact, they are not intended to. The Turnitin report, for example, should only be used as an alert of potential plagiarism; the instructor should use the report to detect which papers require a closer examination because a similarity percentage may not mean that the student copied source material without attribution; they could have included quotes, a correct citation, or an improper citation.

Laboratory Reports

In most instances it is very difficult to determine if the data presented in a laboratory report are genuine or if they have been "cooked" (modified to meet the expectations of the project) or completely fabricated. If the data are too good or too perfect, this can be a clue to the instructor that academic dishonesty may be present. Finding that different laboratory groups have exactly the same results on a laboratory project that typically produces variability in results is another clue that academic dishonesty may be afoot. Turnitin can also be used to detect laboratory report copying because every paper submitted to the website is kept in a central database with which every new paper is compared. Thus, after a couple of years of using the program, teachers will begin to see how many students are simply copying the lab reports from previous years' students!

Online Classes

Given that a recent Google search for "cheating in online classes" yielded 1,920,000 hits, online classes and the potential for academic dishonesty in them appear to be very hot topics. Because the teacher and students may never see each other face to face and the students do much (if not all) of their work on their own, it is very easy for a student to assume another person's identity and then complete the entire course without the instructor being aware of the situation. Hence, the detection of academic dishonesty in online cases may be quite difficult. The fact that it is very difficult for teachers to establish rapport with students in online classes may be a factor that leads to cheating in these environments. These factors have led many researchers to conclude that the percentage or frequency of students who cheat increases as the distance between the students and the classroom increases. Despite the difficulty in detecting cheating in this situation, as you will see later in this chapter, there are some actions that teachers of online classes can take to help deter this behavior.[5]

Even though detection in online classes may be difficult, the magnitude of this problem may not be as extensive as we have implied. In support of this contention, Donna Stuber-McEwen and Phillip Wiseley, researchers from Friends University in Wichita, Kansas, surveyed 243 students who were taking traditional, on-campus classes and students who were enrolled in online classes.[6] Based on the students' anonymous responses that showed more cheating on tests, more plagiarizing, and more aiding/abetting in courses taught on campus, these researchers concluded that students in online classes actually may cheat *less* than students in the traditional classroom. Certainly, this is a topic that will keep researchers busy for several years to come.

Responses to Academic Dishonesty

Once an instance of academic dishonesty has been detected, what type of response should this detection elicit? The best answer to this question probably is "it depends." No, we're not trying to weasel out of giving you an answer. It does depend on who detected the academic dishonesty and what type of evidence is available. We might get different reactions if the infraction was detected by students as opposed to faculty and if the evidence consisted only of an eyewitness account.

113

Students

Students could be among the best allies of the faculty in terms of deterring cheating. They sit in the classes and see cheating on tests and hear other students talk about the schemes they have for plagiarism, and so forth. What do most students do when they have such information? As we have mentioned, their typical response is to do nothing.[7]

Moreover, research has shown that noncheaters believe that it is the teacher's responsibility to stop their classmates from cheating.[8] These students are disappointed and even angry when the teacher does nothing to curtail academic dishonesty. Perhaps if we examine what faculty do when they detect cheating we will be able to understand why this situation exists.

Faculty

Most teachers are aware that cheating is a problem and research on faculty responses to this behavior indicates that a majority of teachers have witnessed cheating in their classes.[9] Unfortunately, few faculty actually do anything about what they have observed. For example, a researcher at Ball State University in Indiana conducted a survey of faculty members. The results indicated that nearly one-quarter of the respondents had ignored incidents of cheating that they had observed. Perhaps even more concerning is the finding that nearly one-third of this number believed that avoiding the problem in this manner was an appropriate and acceptable response. Despite these disturbing figures, we believe it is important to keep in mind that the vast majority of the reported instances of cheating were made by faculty members.

Why does this situation exist? Why do so many faculty members simply ignore this behavior that can and does undermine their chosen profession? After all, isn't it the teacher's responsibility to ensure that all students receive fair and unbiased evaluations? As the following conversation indicates, the fact that confronting students and accusing them of cheating may result in several undesired consequences likely is the root cause of faculty inactivity.

TEACHER 1: A large number of students appeared to be cheating on my exam today.

TEACHER 2: Are you going to do anything about it?

TEACHER 1: I don't want to run the risk of potentially ruining a student's academic career and life beyond college.

TEACHER 2: I know exactly what you mean. When I see cheating, I rarely do anything about it. If the best I can say is that I only "saw" the incident, then there is no hard evidence and it becomes a battle that pits the student's word against mine. In this case, nobody wins and any sort of punishment is very unlikely.

TEACHER 1: I agree completely. Also, trying to take some type of action is likely to involve me in a lengthy process of litigation. Without question, that would be a distasteful occurrence. I simply do not have the time to spend on that process.

In short, many faculty see more compelling reasons to not report than they see for reporting. However, the extent to which these excuses are real or only perceived differs from campus to campus, so schools, colleges, and universities need to make sure that faculty are not adversely affected for "whistle blowing" on student cheating, and they need to work to dispel the myths that faculty perpetuate to discourage new faculty from reporting.

Finally, we probably should stand back from the situation and ask the question "Do faculty members actually detect very much of the cheating that occurs?" Research suggests that the answer is a resounding *no*! For example, with self-reported cheating rates well over 50%, it would seem reasonable to expect that a sizeable number of students would report being caught. However, we know from research reports that the highest reported rate of apprehension is 3%.[10] The typical apprehension rate is approximately 1%. In short, if the behavior is not being detected, then it will not be dealt with.

Penalties

Ultimately, a small minority of the total number of students who cheat will be found guilty and have to face some type of punitive action. Teachers and academic institutions have developed several potential penalties for those students found guilty of academic dishonesty. Among the more common penalties are:

1. failing the assignment (test, term paper, laboratory report, etc.);
2. failing the class;
3. imposing sanctions intended to educate or remediate the student, such as an ethics workshop or academic integrity class;
4. removing the student from the institution temporarily, such as detention or suspension;
5. removing the student permanently from the institution, such as expulsion or dismissal; or,
6. indicating the student's violation with some sort of notation on the student's transcript, such as an XF for the class in which the cheating occurred, or a note indicating the student was suspended or expelled "due to academic dishonesty."

From the viewpoint of teachers and the college or university administration, such penalties may seem appropriately suited for a student who has been academically dishonest.

On the other hand, all students may not be in complete agreement; their views on the appropriate penalties for academic dishonesty are very interesting and informative. A nationwide study of college students asked anonymous respondents what type of punishment they would recommend.[11] Before they suggested specific punishments, many of them indicated that if a student is caught cheating on a test that nothing should be done until after the test. This sentiment suggests that students are sensitive to, and would like to avoid, being humiliated in class. Waiting until after the test period is over also has a potential benefit for the teacher; the testing session is not disrupted and the noncheaters are not disturbed. However, waiting until after the testing session to confront the issue may have some drawbacks. For example, although waiting may avoid humiliating guilty students in front of their classmates, it also can serve as a cue to the class that even though the teacher is aware that cheating is going on, he or she isn't concerned about it. Concerned teachers should, and would, do something about this behavior. Moreover, as all parents are well aware, delayed punishment is never as effective as immediate punishment.

Surprisingly, a large number of the respondents to this survey believed that the best "punishment" was for the teacher to tell the students to "keep your eyes on your own paper." Another sizeable group of respondents believed that an appropriate punishment was for the teacher to take the paper away from the guilty student and allow the student to start over. I'm sure that you will join us in wondering just how effective these "punishments" really are in curtailing academic dishonesty. It is noteworthy that these are the views of students who admitted to cheating.

How about the noncheaters; what type of punishment did they advocate? The most popular punishment for this group of students was for the student who cheated to receive a failing grade on that test or assignment. Considering many students cheat because they are at risk for receiving a failing grade, actually receiving one may not be an effective deterrent by itself. The cost-benefit ratio is highly weighted on the benefit side in such situations. Other popular punishments mentioned by this group included failing the class and expulsion from the university. Clearly, noncheaters are in agreement with the teachers and administrators concerning what they believe are appropriate penalties for cheating.

Short-Term Deterrents

Now that we have considered several of the related issues, let's examine some of the short-term deterrents that might help discourage spur-of-the-moment academic dishonesty, such as cheating on test day, falsifying a laboratory report, or plagiarizing on a term paper. Keep in mind that we will not be describing permanent solutions to the problem of academic dishonesty in this section. We will look at deterrents that often stop cheating in its tracks. The following procedures are more like Band-Aids that are used to stop the bleeding temporarily. We will have a great deal to say about long-term solutions to the problem in subsequent chapters.

Just as there were some disagreements between students and teachers regarding appropriate punishments for academic dishonesty, these two groups also have somewhat divergent opinions concerning short-term deterrents. We will point out these differences as we examine ways to discourage cheating on tests, plagiarism, falsifying laboratory reports, and cheating in online classes.

Tests

There are a sizeable number of options to discourage cheating on tests. Student views provide an interesting insight into how cheating on tests might be discouraged. Their responses to the nationwide survey conducted by Steve Davis and his colleagues[12] indicated that the most *preferred* deterrents to discourage cheating in the classroom were (the following are listed in order of preference):

1. Teachers should use different forms of a test.
2. Teachers should inform the students why they should not cheat.
3. Teachers should arrange the classroom seating so that the students are separated by an empty desk during tests.
4. Teachers should walk up and down the rows during a test.
5. Teachers should constantly watch the students during a test.

Many of the preferred suggestions offered by the students have the potential to be quite effective. For example, using different forms of a test should decrease the frequency of students looking on nearby papers and copying answers. Although using different forms of the test is a potentially effective deterrent, we need to relate an all-too-frequent occurrence that has a serious point, but does poke a little fun at some unsuspecting teachers. We have heard from a substantial number of students that some teachers who use different forms of a test print each of the different forms on a different colored paper. Thus, when the test is completed, all the teacher needs to do is sort the tests by color and he or she is ready to start grading. Unfortunately, it doesn't take students long to realize that if they have a test printed on green paper, then, if they are going to cheat by looking on a nearby paper, they need to be looking at another test printed on green paper. Thus, when faculty members choose to use different forms of the test, they may have to forego ease of sorting for test security, or space students so only "other" versions are within eyesight.

A professor known to one of the authors has a method for both preventing test cheating and catching it when it does happen. First, he creates four different versions of the test. Then, he (along with assistance by others) prepackages the four different versions of the test with marked Scantrons. The Scantrons are marked in two ways. First, he bubbles in the A, B, C, or D under "version" on the front of the Scantron to match the test version with which the Scantron is packaged. Then, he codes the version on the back of each Scantron as well, in a way that is not obvious to the unaware user. When the student erases the test version bubble on the front in order to cheat off a neighbor, it is easy enough to confront them with their act.

Likewise, separating students by an empty desk often discourages students from looking on nearby papers; however, the crowded nature of contemporary classrooms may preclude this alternative. Another deterrent, walking up and down the rows and watching the students while they are taking a test, emphasizes the need for teachers to be vigilant during the testing situation. Certainly, vigilance is a key deterrent. We have already seen that faculty who are not vigilant or who leave the room are sending a message that many students interpret as not caring whether students cheat. On the other hand, vigilance is difficult to implement in a classroom containing several hundred students; clearly, more than one proctor will be needed to observe the students during the test. If sufficient proctors are available, they also should check student IDs to make sure that the students entering the room are actually on the class roster and that the picture on the ID matches the face of the student who is there to take the test.

Thus, the leaders of the educational institutions have some role to play in this as well – packed classrooms and unstaffed examinations create cheating temptations that are too hard for many young people (under stress and pressure) to resist. Such institutional problems are commonplace in large, public universities, and these issues emerge even more predominantly in times of financial downturn as faculty positions are cut but enrollment increases in order to close the expenditure-revenue gap. One thing that institutional leaders could do to help faculty in a cost-effective way is to arrange final examinations in a large arena so that students in different subject areas could be seated next to each other, rather than having 300 introductory chemistry students sitting shoulder to shoulder in one overstuffed classroom. The University of Toronto, in Ontario, Canada, and most likely others, do this.

Another cost-effective way to reduce opportunities for cheating is the "blue book exchange." Colleges and universities often create opportunities for cheating with their cost-saving measures, such as requiring students to provide their own blue books for their exams. Of course, some students use such an opportunity to pre-write answers or information in their blue book, and then tear out those pages before turning the book in. With little significant investment up front, a department could buy a set of blue books, one for each test taker, and stamp each blue book with some sort of unique indicator (e.g., the department's name stamp). Then, when students enter the exam room, they turn in their blue books and receive one of the department's in return. The department, then, can check those blue books (to make sure they are free of information), stamp them, and hand them out to the next set of exam takers, and the cycle continues.

What about informing students why they should not cheat? Will this announcement be an effective deterrent? If the announcement includes refreshing the students' memory concerning the penalties for cheating, then it may reduce cheating during the ensuing test period. This reduction in cheating, most likely, will be most effective with "impulse cheaters" who do not cheat on a regular basis and might be tempted by the sight of an uncovered answer sheet. As the quote from a hard-core cheater that opened this chapter suggests, these students are going to cheat no matter what!

According to the student respondents, the less preferred deterrents included:

1. the teacher simply announcing "do not cheat";
2. having assigned seats;
3. having an all-essay exam;
4. requiring the students to leave their belongings outside the classroom during the test;
5. embarrassing students in front of their classmates.

As with the more preferred deterrents, these less-preferred deterrents have both pros and cons associated with them. For example, simply announcing "do not cheat" to students likely will not have much, if any, effect on academic dishonesty if the students have devised a plan to cheat before the test or if they have convinced themselves that what they are doing is not cheating. At best this announcement may deter spur-of-the-moment, impulsive cheating in some students.

Although having assigned seats may discourage premeditated collaborative cheating, it certainly will not discourage students from taking cheat sheets and other unauthorized materials to the exam or from looking on their neighbors' papers.

121

On the other hand, two reasons may have prompted students to put "having all-essay tests" on their less-preferred list. First, most of us can remember how the thought of an impending essay test struck fear in our hearts; tests, such as multiple-choice and true–false, that allowed us the ability to choose among several answers always seemed easier. Second, students may have put all-essay tests in the less preferred category because it is much more difficult, if not impossible, to get answers from another student or by looking on a neighbor's test paper during an essay test. Despite their excellent potential to curb academic dishonesty, the extra time and effort required to grade essay exams have not resulted in their widespread use. Imagine having to grade 300+ essay exams!

Having students leave their belongings outside the classroom during the exam is an interesting inclusion on the students' less-preferred list. It also can be viewed in two ways. Some students may be expressing a genuine concern that their belongings may be stolen if they are left unattended outside the classroom. On the other hand, for students who intend to cheat on a test, being forced to leave their belongings outside the classroom decreases their ability to access un-authorized materials during the test. Of course, faculty can address the first concern by having students leave their belongings in full view of the class at the front of the room, not outside the room.

Instructors cited the same preferred deterrents to cheating as the students, and then some! For example, many faculty do not allow students to bring bottled water to class. As we have seen, some students who are determined to cheat will remove the label from the bottle, write answers on the label, and then replace the label on the bottle. Likewise, many teachers do not allow students to wear ball caps (answers have been written on the bill) or sunglasses (answers have been written on the inside of the lenses) during tests. Several faculty members have told us that they have learned to be wary of students with no apparent hearing difficulties who suddenly appear to take a test wearing a hearing enhancement device. Moreover, many teachers have banned programmable calculators and similar electronic devices from the testing situation.

On Campus

"In a sign of increasing concern about cheating, the nation's top business schools will soon require a high-tech identity check for standardized admissions tests . . . Palm-vein scanning . . . will begin next month in Korea and India . . .[to] target [sic] 'proxy' test taking, a fraud in which applicants hire high-scoring imposters to take the exam in their place."

From *The Wall Street Journal* (2008, July 22), "Business schools try palm scans to finger cheats," by John Hechinger

---

Certainly faculty have developed numerous techniques that they hope will reduce cheating on tests in their classes. Reducing plagiarism also has received considerable attention.

Plagiarism

The following conversation between two teachers should give you some ideas concerning combating plagiarism.

TEACHER 1: I've been plagued with a rash of students plagiarizing recently. How about you?

TEACHER 2: I've had the same experience.

TEACHER 1: What are you doing to try to control it?

TEACHER 2: I'm trying to design writing assignments that preclude, or at least discourage, plagiarism. This is the best defense against plagiarism that I've found.

TEACHER 1: How does this work? What do you do? It sounds like it is easier said than done.

TEACHER 2: I agree that it may sound somewhat difficult, but with some practice you quickly will become an old pro. Some of the specifics of my writing projects that I use to combat plagiarism include making my assignments personal and having the students relate the topic they choose to their own lives. This keeps the students from purchasing a more general paper from the internet or a local paper writer.

TEACHER 1: That makes sense to me. What else do you do?

TEACHER 2: I require that my students turn in draft copies of their work during the semester so I can see the paper take shape and develop. I also require that my students turn in an outline of their writing project during the semester. Also, I devote at least one class period to working on the writing project. During this class session I can circulate among the students and, while I am helping them with their projects, I can take notice of which students aren't on track with their projects and may be tempted to plagiarize.

Each of the procedures described by Teacher 2 has a unique ability to reduce plagiarism. For example, as noted, making the assignment very personal (e.g., relating it directly to their own life) discourages students from buying a paper from an internet supplier, a friend, or a local paper writer.

Likewise, the intent of having the students turn in rough drafts or portions of the assignment throughout the term is to keep them from simply purchasing a complete paper near the end of the term and thereby avoiding working on the project themselves. Unfortunately, this approach does not keep students from buying a paper early in the term and then dissecting it and submitting the required section(s) during the term. Having the students turn in an outline of the various sections of the paper throughout the term has the advantage of not allowing them to simply dissect a purchased paper. In order to prepare an outline, the student has to know and understand the topic.

If teachers can devote a class period to working on the term paper, they can directly observe the materials that the students have gathered and that the project is taking shape. Of course, if the term-paper work session is announced beforehand, then the students who are guilty of plagiarizing likely will not attend. Such absences can be a signal to the teacher to examine the papers of these students closely. Despite the potential effectiveness of these deterrents, plagiarism will not be completely eliminated; teachers must be vigilant!

Even the use of plagiarism detection software, like Turnitin, does not eliminate all plagiarism. At one of the author's universities, and we are sure many others, students continue to submit plagiarized material to Turnitin – that is how they get caught! So, a group of students who had been caught for plagiarizing were asked if they understood what Turnitin does, and they said "yes". They were asked, "Why do you still submit a paper with copied material?" And to that they essentially replied, "We lose our minds," or "I thought I paraphrased it sufficiently to not be plagiarism." Students seem to "lose their minds" when they are down to the final hour and have not yet finished their paper. These students reported that they had written most of their papers, properly cited the material they had used thus far, but felt that they could not simply turn in the paper as it was if it was under the teacher-specified page limit. So, feeling obligated to fill all of the pages, they copied and pasted the remainder of the paper. Teachers, then, may want to think about how they can reduce this page limit obsession, perhaps by helping the students focus on quality of the writing rather than quantity.

Laboratory Reports

The nature of the laboratory assignment will determine what teachers can and cannot do to deter cheating. If the assignment consists of the students gathering data on their own time outside the classroom, then sensitivity to the data and the specifics of the report may be the only effective deterrent. Most undergraduates do not understand why fabricating data is considered to be such an offense in the academy. Thus, faculty need to socialize students into the research culture and draw clear comparisons between the practice of student labs and the practice of "real" labs and of truth seeking. On a more practical level, if students are aware that their teacher reads each report thoroughly and that they will be questioned about unusual procedures (e.g., completing the assignment in an exceptionally short period of time), methodology (e.g., how the participants acted during the testing session), and data (e.g., why there were or were not many extreme scores), the amount of data cooking and fabrication likely will decrease.

If the laboratory is held in a regular classroom at a scheduled time, then the teacher has more control over the situation. Student progress with the assignment can be monitored and instances of academic dishonesty detected and dealt with.

Online Classes

The Connecticut Distance Learning Consortium (www.ctdlc.org) has proposed several steps that teachers can take to curtail cheating in online classes. Many of these suggestions involve having the students engage in an activity or project. Among their suggestions are:

1. use standard testing instruments (e.g., multiple-choice, matching, essay, etc.) for self-assessment. These tests do not count toward the students' grades;
2. require active participation in online discussions;
3. use reports and projects to assess learning and assign grades;
4. in agreement with our discussion of deterring plagiarism, they suggest that portions of the research paper or project should be due throughout the course.

Although these practices may help deter cheating in online classes, the fact that the teacher may never see the students in a face-to-face situation does make it more difficult to determine who is actually doing the work that is being submitted.

On the other hand, we already reviewed a report that indicates that students in online classes may engage in academic dishonesty less frequently than students in regular on-campus classes. In evaluating their project, the researchers noted that online classes may not lead students to engage in panic or spur-of-the-moment cheating as readily as do crowded classrooms on campus.[13] They also noted that the online students were older than the on-campus students; this result supports the finding that older students are less likely to engage in academic dishonesty.[14]

In the News

The renewed Higher Education Act contains "a small paragraph that could lead distance-education institutions to require spy cameras in their students' homes. It sounds Orwellian, but the paragraph . . . is actually about clamping down on cheating . . . [because it is requiring that institutions offering online education] must prove that an enrolled student is the same person who does the work."

From *The Chronicle of Higher Education* (2008, July 25), "New systems keep a close eye on students at home," by Andrea L. Foster. Retrieved July 25, 2008, from www.chronicle.com

---

Effectiveness of Short-Term Deterrents

Have the multitude of short-term deterrents been successful in discouraging cheating? Unfortunately, without any relevant data that speak directly to this issue, it is very difficult to answer this question. On the one hand, it is arguable that these short-term deterrents have been effective, especially with students who might have engaged in panic or spur-of-the-moment cheating.

However, very low rates of detection combined with minimal (at best) punishment, suggest that their effectiveness is definitely limited, especially with habitual cheaters. Likewise, the high levels of academic dishonesty that we examined earlier suggest that these deterrents have had limited effectiveness, at best. In this context, you should recall the student comment that opened this chapter.

Table 5.1 The short-term deterrents that may work for specific cheating techniques

Techniques	Short-term deterrents
Test cheating	
Copying off another student	Space students out so it is difficult to see other exams
	Use multiple versions of the exam so students at least copy the wrong answers!
Student collusion (such as pre-arranged signals)	Sufficient proctors to observe behaviors
Using cheat sheets or other unauthorized aids	Require students to leave all belongings at the front of the room
Technological assistance (such as recording answers on mp3 players, text messaging, or storing answers in calculators or PDAs)	Have the institution block out the WiFi signal in the room during the examination
Filling out Blue Books ahead of time	Implement the Blue Book Exchange – students bring in a blue book and get a stamped blue book in return
Exam proxies	Check ID cards against class roster
Using old examinations	Make old exam papers available to *all* students if not considered cheating; otherwise, inform students if it is
Paper cheating	
Plagiarism	Use Turnitin or other plagiarism detection software
Buying pre-written papers	Require drafts, read them & provide feedback

Table 5.1 *(cont'd)*

Techniques	Short-term deterrents
Copying former student's papers	Change writing prompts yearly; ideally, make the writing assignments personal and interesting (rather than generic)
Laboratory cheating	
Falsifying lab data	Test students on lab procedures rather than assessing ability on lab reports
Copying old lab reports	Use Turnitin
Fabrication/fraud	
Altering graded exams for re-grades	Photocopy all exams, random exams, or certain pages of all exams (i.e., pages with the questions most students will get incorrect) before returning them Closely mark the wrong answers in a way that makes it difficult for students to change Require exams to be written in ink

"Nothing short of dismemberment will stop me from cheating."

Comments such as this one suggest that developing long-term deterrents might produce more fruitful results. Before we turn to those long-term deterrents in the next chapter, we offer a summary of the last two chapters by listing in Table 5.1 the cheating techniques and the appropriate mechanisms that can be implemented to thwart the success of them.

Chapter 6

Long-Term Deterrents

Development of Individual and Institutional Integrity

When we consider . . . the university expectations, national policies, community and parental desires, and the school factors that seem so difficult to reform, we may shrug our shoulders in defeat. The system is too entrenched, too complex, and too vast to make significant changes. Yet, when we listen to what students want from their education, what they believe they need to be productive citizens and to feel genuinely successful, we may begin to see possible alternatives to the kinds of schools and systems of competition exemplified [in today's society].[1]

We began the first chapter by posing a question and providing an unsatisfying answer: "What's the problem? Everyone does it." In the second chapter, we showed the depth of the contradiction since we now know two things: just about every student does cheat at some point in their educational years and yet most students do not cheat all the time. We know why students cheat: "students . . . feel pressures to get better grades, view cheating as not very serious conduct, perceive the gains to outweigh the risks, and consider friends to be somewhat tolerant of this activity," teachers and parents are slow to confront cheating, and there are "frequent opportunities for cheating."[2]

Given the relative acceptability of cheating among students, it is still remarkable that there is as much academic honesty as there is. The challenge is to build on academic honesty and reduce the incidence of cheating: "The main task of an institution is not to detect cheaters, but rather create an environment where academic dishonesty is socially unacceptable."[3]

We believe that cheating can be maintained at an acceptable level of corruption if we can move academic misconduct from merely "disagreeable" in the minds of students, parents, teachers, and administrators to socially unacceptable and morally reprehensible. Steven Pinker, a psychologist at Harvard University, refers to this work as activating a "moralization switch."[4] Pinker and others[5] believe that that there is flexibility in how society decides what is moral and what is social convention or normative (and therefore only disagreeable). He notes how smoking has gone in recent years from disagreeable to virtually immoral and how other behaviors have been pushed from "moral failings" to "lifestyle choices." It seems plausible, then, that the academic behaviors currently seen as merely "disagreeable" methods that students use to be "successful" can be reframed as cheating and a moral failing for both the individual and the educational institution.

How might this be done?

First we should probably say how it *cannot* be done. Despite the pleas of many teachers and faculty for harsh sanctioning, we do not think the tide of corruption can be stemmed by simply evicting student cheaters from the school. For too long we have depended on the disciplinary method for ridding our schools of cheaters and clearly the method is failing us; despite the suspension or even expulsion of student cheaters, cheating continues. Why? Most student cheating is not caught, so the threat of sanction does little to deter most students. Many students, as we saw in Chapter 2, do not perceive their behaviors *as* cheating, and therefore threats of harsh sanctions for cheating will not deter those students. Cheating is largely situational, as we saw in Chapter 3, and so expelling the few students who are caught cheating does not fix one of the primary sources of the problem. Finally, though sanctions should be part of the solution (to shift the cost-benefit ratio of student cheating), they primarily affect the one student who was sanctioned and therefore do not address the underlying causes of the problem which are embedded within the educational system.

We maintain there are two primary, and better, methods for deterring student cheating in the long term and creating a culture of integrity: moral development, primarily of students and teachers, and the institutionalization of integrity in educational organizations. We will sketch out each, show how they interact, and then, in the next chapter, shift our attention away from students to see how the conversations and stories of parents, teachers, educational administrators, and public citizens are so important in building academic honesty and a culture of integrity on our campuses.

Moral Development: Of Individuals and Institutions

The values wars debate described in the first chapter provides the backdrop for our discussion here of individual development as a long-term deterrent. We argue that there is a role for education to play in the moral and ethical development of its students because, "without a well-rounded, balanced, educated citizenry having high standards, ethics and morals, a nation cannot hope to maintain or advance its position in the world."[6] Though the values debates got caught up in concerns over "whose" values should be taught, this need not be the case. We suggest that educational institutions can reduce student cheating and create an ethical, educated workforce by teaching universal values, developing moral reasoning, and honing ethical decision-making.

William Kibler, now Vice President for Student Affairs at Mississippi State University, and colleagues were the first to suggest attending to student moral development as a long-term deterrent to student academic misconduct.[7] In particular, Kibler and co-authors focused on the applicability of cognitive moral development theories which advocate the development of ethical reasoning so students can more effectively resolve moral dilemmas. Specifically, cognitive moral development theories suggest that people gradually develop their ability to resolve moral and ethical dilemmas as they gain "understanding of cooperative relationships" through experiences and interactions in which they "encounter different perspectives and roles" and face "moral conflict" which demonstrates "the inadequacy of lower stages of reasoning."[8] Thus, as students progress through educational levels in which they gain experience and learn about multiple viewpoints, it is likely that students will develop their moral reasoning abilities. In fact, the experience of a student being caught for cheating can be used as a moment to work on moral development. However, this moment should not be left to chance, and it should not be assumed that learning from experience will occur through normal maturation; schools and colleges have a responsibility to create intentional experiences for the students to develop ethical reasoning skills and moral judgment.

On Campus

The Rutland Institute for Ethics at Clemson University is an exemplary source of information on teaching ethics and developing integrity among students, faculty, and community members. The Institute offers multiple ethical programs, including corporate ethical training and ethics contests for undergraduates, intended to teach students, faculty, and community members about ethics and integrity. The goal of the Institute extends beyond stimulating ethical conversations to actually teaching ethical practices, ethical decision-making, and ethical conflict resolutions. Visit the Institute's website for more information www.clemson.edu/ethics/index.php.

Elizabeth Nuss and others caution, however, that the development of sophisticated moral judgment does not necessarily lead to moral action – the relationship between the two is complex and situationally variable. Why might this be? Individual choice of actions is influenced by interests and needs that often conflict with each other and the moral high ground. Though a student, for example, may judge unauthorized collaboration as morally wrong because the professor strictly prohibited it, students may choose to collaborate anyway because they know it will improve their learning, they'll produce better work, and it will level the playing field (because most of their classmates are working with each other). Alternatively students choose to work with a friend on the assignment because they are in danger of failing and need that friend's help.

So, what can educational institutions do to help students first recognize a behavior as moral (honest) or immoral (cheating) and then act according to that judgment when faced with an ethical dilemma? Moral development theorists suggest that schools could attend to developing in students four components of moral action: moral sensitivity, moral judgment, moral motivations, and moral behavior.[9] Table 6.1 describes the characteristics of each of the four components and lists possible educational institution interventions. To develop each component, schools, colleges, and universities need to be intentional and willing to intervene on the moral matter of integrity versus cheating.

Table 6.1 Institutional interventions that could develop each component of moral action

Moral component	Educational institution intervention
Moral sensitivity Interpreting the situation as one involving moral questions or dilemmas	Have a clearly written and fair policy that delineates what the community considers ethical and unethical conduct. Be frank with students that they will face moral/ethical dilemmas while trying to live by the ethical code. For example, do I follow the rules even though I know I could get a better grade if I don't? Should I be loyal to my friend who needs my help on an independent assignment or loyal to the school (and its rules)?

Table 6.1 (*cont'd*)

Moral component	Educational institution intervention
Identifying all of the possibilities for action	Engage the students in open discussion and dialogue about all of the possibilities they have for action when facing moral dilemmas. Students at lower stages of reasoning will tend to dichotomize their choices; help them see all of the possibilities. For example, are there ethical ways to help a friend in need, like encouraging him to talk with the teacher about his struggles?
Considering the impact of choices on others	Clearly explain why the community considers certain behaviors unethical – what values do the behaviors undermine? How do they harm others?

Moral judgment

Of all the possible choices for action, determining the ideal course	A clear ethical code or academic integrity policy can help students know what the institution considers the ideal choice. The code or policy should spell out not just what students shouldn't do, but what they should do instead of cheating (e.g., go to a writing center for writing help, rather than copy and paste).
Determining which choice is the right choice	Individual teachers should also make it clear what are the right choices in their particular class and with particular academic assignments. Teach universal values such as those prescribed by the CharacterCounts! and academic integrity movements.[1]
Recognizing the reasons for doing the right thing	Create different interventions for students at different moral reasoning stages. For example, students at earlier stages of moral development will respond best to published rules and clear sanctions

Table 6.1 *(cont'd)*

Moral component	Educational institution intervention

(i.e., costs) for engaging in academic misconduct. Therefore,

1 have a clearly written procedure for punishing academic misconduct and spell out the costs (e.g., sanctions) for choosing behaviors that are considered unethical by the community.

However, students further along in their moral development may respond to appeals to higher order principles like fairness and equity. Therefore,

2 have open discussions about how academic integrity is in the students' best self-interests because academic integrity protects the value of their diploma/degree and it is fair;
3 have an open dialogue about the ethical code or policy as the "golden rule"; it is about being a good person and maintaining values like trust, loyalty, and respect in the relationships between students and teachers;
4 discuss with students the ethical code as the duties with which they have agreed to abide while being members of the academic community and that acting in line with the code protects the institution against corruption and a bad reputation.

Moral motivations

Choosing the ideal action over alternatives — Make academic integrity more profitable than academic misconduct; publicize the costs of engaging in academic misconduct.

Table 6.1 *(cont'd)*

Moral component	Educational institution intervention
Prioritizing values	Ensure that the institution exemplifies the values that students are expected to prioritize. Brand the school as an academic integrity school; make academic integrity popular and "trendy" as a value.
Moral behavior	
Engaging in the ideal action despite frustration, lack of support, and other obstacles	Create an environment (structures, procedures, norms, etc.) that supports ethical decision-making and moral action. Reduce opportunities for cheating and obstacles to academic integrity (e.g., opaque instructions and lax testing environments), especially for younger students who will take the risks if there are great benefits.[2]

[1] The six pillars of character in the CharacterCounts! movement and the five fundamental values in the academic integrity movement align with the five values that, according to Pinker, are universal and found in every culture: (1) do not harm others; (2) be fair, that is, "reciprocate favors, reward benefactors and punish cheaters"; (3) be loyal to a community through "sharing and solidarity among its members and conformity to its norms"; (4) "defer to legitimate authorities and . . . respect people with high status"; and (5) "exalt purity, cleanliness and sanctity while loathing defilement, contamination and carnality" (p. 36).

[2] Brody, Jane, E., 2007 (December 18), "Teenage risks, and how to avoid them," *The New York Times* (D7).

In tandem, parents and societal members must give schools the lee-way to do so, rather than fight them in continuing values wars.

We would like to expand on five interventions not normally dis-cussed in the academic integrity literature but integral to helping students develop moral sensitivity, judgment, and motivation to act with integrity: helping students with "self-binding"; teaching students how to resolve ethical dilemmas; increasing the profitability of academic integrity; branding academic integrity; and attending to the ethical conduct of teachers.

Helping Students "Self-bind" Their Cheating Selves

Helping students learn how to "bind" their cheating self in favor of their honest self may not be as fanciful as it may appear at first glance. "Researchers now believe, to varying degrees, that each of us is a community of competing selves."[10] If that is so, it can go far in explaining why students may cheat even when knowing it is wrong. And it may explain why most students do not cheat most of the time. Paul Bloom, reflecting on psychological studies at Yale 80 years ago, states that students who have a "propensity to cheat at sports" may not cheat in the classroom.[11] "This sticking lack of consistency" means "the different selves can be brought to the fore by different situations."[12] But it also suggests that these "competing selves" can be trained to "self-bind," that is, find ways to "block" the self which can be predicted to emerge in a given situation; "self-binding means that the dominant self schemes against the person it might potentially become."[13]

In his 2008 article in *The Atlantic Monthly*, Paul Bloom gives multiple examples of how self-binding can work by structuring situations to avoid temptations. One of Bloom's examples is "to demand a room with an empty minibar" to avoid the temptation to nibble while traveling.[14] But we all know, and Bloom confirms, "that the problem is that the self you're trying to bind has resources of its own" to confound the best of plans.[15] The difficulties of self-binding are legion, but could it apply to the effort to reduce student cheating? Imagine the following interior conversation:

SELF: I know that every time I get behind on my math homework, I rely on my friend, Harry, to "lend" me the right answers. This is cheating, and I feel bad about it. I have to find a way to avoid that situation

COMPETING SELF:	Get real – you know you don't like math, and you will procrastinate as usual. Besides, cutting corners on homework is not that bad.
SELF:	I can get away with this now in high school but I have to take the SAT next year, and I may want to major in sciences in college. I'd better find a better way to get this done.
COMPETING SELF:	Sure, you'll give it a try but you'll start to fall behind as soon as you start rehearsals for the play in the spring.
SELF:	Actually, the more work I seem to have, the more I seem to get done. Maybe I should just set it up to do that 15 minutes of math homework before I turn on the computer each evening – that will be my reward for getting it done.
COMPETING SELF:	I'll believe it when I see it.
SELF:	Well – you're going to see it.

Whether or not the student is going to be successful may be less important than the recognition of a problem and a commitment to resolve it. Moving from small successes to larger ones is important, however, and we all know that building good habits is a key to self improvement. "How to" books seem to sell well. More research will need to be done on how to encourage self-binding on the matter of confronting student cheating. Self-improvement needs to be more than dieting and exercise. Stimulating more studies of self-improvement as applied to the habits of supporting academic integrity should be one point of emphasis in dealing with the epidemic of student cheating.

Teaching Students How to Resolve Ethical Dilemmas

Asking students to "self-bind" so that they choose the moral action and not cheat when completing their academic work is not as simple as it sounds; "even individuals who have achieved a high moral development stage may not recognize cheating as a moral problem and, consequently, their behavior would not be influenced by the moral aspects of the act."[16] The literature on academic integrity is replete with acknowledgments of the complexity of the issue and the ethical dilemmas that arise for students.[17] Ethical dilemmas arise for students because the decision to "cheat" is not always a right-versus-wrong choice.

Clearly, when a student is thinking about hacking into the school's computer system to change grades or gain early access to a test, the student should be able to interpret the situation as one involving a moral or ethical line which he is considering crossing.[18] However, sometimes the student is facing a right-versus-right choice when considering cheating. For example, it is the "right" choice for a student to help a friend with a class assignment because his friend is an international student who is in danger of being deported because of poor grades, but it is also the "right" choice for the student to follow the teacher's rules to complete the assignment independently. It is the role of the educational institution, the parent, and other morally developed adults to help students develop the ability to recognize this situation and multiple others (see sidebar) as ethical dilemmas and then to think through all of the possible courses of action that could honor both "rights."

On Campus

Beyond the dilemma of loyalty (to a friend) and truth (to the teacher), students will routinely struggle with other rights-versus-rights dilemmas as they progress through school. For example, students may be pushed to reconcile their self-interests with the interests of the school community, as when a student is asked to sacrifice a good grade for the honest completion of an assignment. Or when the student is forced to choose between reporting students for cheating (justice) and having sympathy for the students who need a good grade to maintain their financial aid (mercy).

Pinker himself said it best: "The optimistic proposal that our moral sense, though shaped by evolution to overvalue self, kin and clan, can propel us on a path of moral progress, as our reasoning forces us to generalize it to larger and larger circles of sentient beings."[19] In considering the other stakeholders, the student in our illustration could choose several ethical ways to help their friend while abiding by the rules of the classroom – for example, encouraging the friend to ask the teacher for help, tutoring the friend but not giving them the answers, or asking the teacher if they can work together given the circumstances. We need to acknowledge that "students (teachers, administrators, and parents) live in the midst of competing values and attitudes and their 'pro-institutional attitudes' (portraying cheating as a negative behavior) may be weakened by adherence to other social 'loyalties.' "[20]

To help students develop the ability to identify moral dilemmas and choose the right course of action, we must provide students with the opportunities to confront and struggle with these dilemmas (as well as struggle with complex thinking) by supporting and challenging them through the "cognitive disequilibrium [that arises when facing] ethical dilemma situations."[21] The ambitious achievement orientation of today's students and their desire to "succeed" rather than to learn must be balanced by allowing students to "make significant personal decisions [and] to take responsibility for themselves."[22] For example, we ask students not to cheat because it is not "fair," but yet tests, other academic assignments, and teachers are not always fair. Because students are achievement-oriented and their moral reasoning skills are undeveloped, they may use the lack of fairness as an excuse for cheating. Educational institutions and parents have a responsibility to teach our students how they can ethically respond to unfair evaluations and teachers. Schools should also have in place policies and procedures to help parents and students do just that.

However, despite our work on moral and ethical development, students will still cheat. And such cheating, if maintained at an acceptable level of corruption, is "normative and (from a developmental perspective) necessary and to be expected. By pushing the

On Campus

Both the Josephson Institute (through its CharacterCounts! Program) and the Institute for Global Ethics offer curriculum ideas and lesson plans for K-12 teachers who wish to teach students about ethics and integrity. See their websites at www.charactercounts.org and www.globalethics.org.

boundaries and testing the limits of moral behavior within a 'safe' academic setting, students may actually be priming and reinforcing their own understanding of moral behavior by ... learning the reward and punishment schema that accompany such behaviors."[23]

This normal testing behavior does not end once the student receives the high school diploma, as most college and university professors would like to believe. Thus, we can and should expect cheating to occur by college students and not overreact when we see it, that is, bemoan the immorality of the entire generation of students or cry foul and take it personally (which can be difficult for teachers not to). We should, on the other hand, confront the cheating (rather than look the other way) and respond in ways that can facilitate the student's development.

In assistance to faculty, campus procedures to resolve allegations of misconduct

> should provide the student with an opportunity to confront the ethical implications of their behavior, gain a better understanding of the roles and responsibilities of students and faculty within the academic community, develop an appreciation of the values associated with effective scholarship, and gain exposure to forms of moral reasoning they can comprehend and which are likely to stimulate their development.[24]

This means that an effective long-term deterrent to cheating and education corruption may *not* be the eviction of offenders from the school (i.e., through suspension or expulsion). Rather, schools may want to consider enrolling students in educational opportunities to learn from their experience. Many universities and colleges, for example, require that students complete an academic integrity seminar in which they explore ideas of ethics and academic integrity.[25] Research needs to be conducted on the effectiveness of such seminars, but anecdotal experience suggests that they can positively impact a student's conceptions of academic integrity (see the box below).

On Campus

Students who completed an academic integrity seminar made the following comments when asked to "provide any additional comments you would like to make about the seminar":

- "I believe this seminar should be required on the first quarter of all entering students – freshman, transfers, or otherwise."
- "I felt that the group discussions were a good learning experience for us to gain insight on the rights/wrongs about academic integrity."
- "I really loved this seminar and I've learned very valuable lesson for my life. *Thank you so much.*"
- "It was a great experience to go through the seminar. I thought it would be a drag; however, I enjoyed not only the class but the assignments as well."
- "It was a very comfortable environment to talk with peers."
- "It was insightful and would be helpful to other students."
- "It was very, very good. The small group atmosphere helped us to open up. I am glad I took part in this. I will never forget this experience."
- "This incident definitely built my character and I am positive that I have learned from this and it will help me be a better person."

Increasing the Profitability of Academic Integrity

If you recall, fairness is a core value articulated in both the character education and academic integrity movements. Fairness refers to clarity of standards, consistency, and predictability, though academics like Pinker suggest that fairness also connotes offering rewards for "good behavior." Many schools, including those with honor codes, do attempt to highlight the rewards of academic honesty in terms of moral reputation and as an asset to potential employers of graduates, but the whole notion of profitability of academic honesty needs to be better established because "people who do not recognize cheating as a moral issue resort to other decision-making mechanisms such as relying on in-group norms or on ad hoc utilitarian reasoning, where one contemplates whether the benefits outweigh the costs."[26] And, contrary to what one may think, students (especially those in high school and undergraduates in college) do not enter into what adults think are "risky" behaviors because they fail to see the risks, but because they calculate that the benefits are worth any potential risks.[27]

If we wish to convey academic integrity as the "right" choice of action, then, we have to work to ensure that not only are the costs high for choosing academic misconduct but the benefits are higher for choosing academic integrity. In other words, academic integrity has to be profitable for the individual student, teacher, and the institution as a whole.[28] Yet, in many of our schools and colleges, academic integrity may not currently be profitable. There are immediate rewards for students who engage in academic misconduct in terms of higher grades and there are costs to teachers and schools for upholding academic integrity in terms of time not spent on other activities for which they are rewarded or recognized (for example, research, athletic programs, diversity).[29] So, how can academic integrity be more profitable and thus easier to choose as the "right" choice when there are multiple options for action available?

Perhaps the most effective way to increase the perceived profitability of academic integrity is through eliciting the help of the very

On Campus

Somehow, advocates of diversity, internationalization, and sustainability have managed to convince colleges and universities (in the United States, at least) of the profitability of those initiatives. Certainly a focus on sustainability *can* be profitable to campuses (when they save money on electricity, for example), but diversity and internationalization efforts can *cost* campuses enormous sums of money and human resources. So, how were these initiatives able to spread so widely and become a strategic priority on campuses across America? The answer is that they are *profitable* – the large majority of society, potential students, and potential faculty want colleges and universities to be diverse, internationalized, and sustainable, and therefore making them so means "profit."

Thus, in regard to academic integrity, the key will be convincing society, potential students, potential faculty and administrators that they *want* to be associated with a school, college, or university that is known for its integrity (and not just for its diversity, international components, and sustainable practices).

people that students think want the high grades – colleges, employers, and graduate/professional schools. If high school students cheat for college, then colleges need to make it profitable for students to repudiate cheating and advocate academic integrity. If college students cheat for careers, then employers and graduate/professional schools need to make it profitable for colleges to repudiate cheating and advocate academic integrity. Perhaps, for example, students can be rewarded admission points for clean disciplinary records and contribution to their school's culture of integrity by, for example, serving on the school's honor council or stepping up as a "whistle-blower" on academic corruption in their school. In addition, high schools and colleges could be ranked for their efforts to create cultures of integrity (see the piece on institutionalization later in the chapter) and students coming from highly ranked "integrity schools" should be viewed more favorably when applying for admission or a job.

Within schools and colleges, administrators also need to work on making academic integrity more profitable than academic misconduct. Teachers should not only be supported in their monitoring of academic misconduct and the teaching of the five fundamental academic integrity values, but also rewarded for creating cultures of integrity within their own classrooms and for developing the moral reasoning and behaviors of their students. Some ideas include:

- considering a teacher's attention to academic integrity as part of the tenure and promotion process;
- if a teacher has committed significant effort to reduce cheating and enhance academic integrity, the expectations for other tenure requirements (for example, the number or quality of publications) during that same period could be reduced;
- teachers who report cheating in a given semester should be assured that any outlier negative student evaluations that they receive will be factored out of their overall performance; and,
- campuses could give out awards and publically recognize faculty who promote academic integrity.

Other methods directed at students could be implemented to make academic integrity more profitable:

- students would see that they profit more from an honestly earned C than a dishonestly earned A if the school ranked classes by their "integrity value." This could be done by indicating on transcripts which grades were earned in classes led by teachers who emphasized academic integrity and reported cheating so that outside readers would know which grades were honestly earned and were thus more accurate reflections of ability and achievement;

147

- campuses could give out awards and publically recognize entire classes who uphold the honor code or students who champion academic integrity on campus; and,
- students who take more "integrity classes" could receive some sort of honor at graduation or an indication on their transcript.

As we develop in students the ability to see cheating as morally reprehensible and to choose academic integrity over cheating despite the sacrifice of desirables, we can help students by making the costs of cheating and the rewards of academic integrity higher. While we aim to develop intellectually empowered moral citizens, we can provide them with self-interest motivations along the way. One way to do this, to increase the profitability of academic integrity, is to "brand" it.

Branding Academic Integrity

A promising way to motivate students to choose academically honest actions over dishonest actions may be to have students and others identify the "integrity school" as a desirable "brand." Branding creates or shapes an identity for an institution[30] to link the institution "with what people take pride in, what they value as a society, and what they identify with."[31] Honor-code schools such as the University of Virginia and the Air Force Academy may be examples of successful attempts to brand academic integrity; most students and alumni of these two schools take pride in their honor codes and cite them as an added value for the institution. For most other schools, the business of education has led to branding only those aspects that lead to increased revenue, usually successful sports programs or logos that sell tickets and school merchandise. It is astonishing how important the business model is to education today, particularly higher education, yet academic integrity itself is rarely accounted for its possible economic value.

As we argued in Chapter 1, academic integrity ensures the meaningfulness of a diploma or degree; without honest evaluations and assessments, the integrity of the educational enterprise is corrupted and the usefulness of certification is lost. Though the definitions and processes associated with academic integrity may be debated, students, teachers and administrators benefit from a school being known as "integrous."[32] And, it is doubtful that any student or teacher would want to be associated with a school that is known for being dishonest or a "cheating school." Thus, it seems likely that academic integrity can hold some economic value and is a concept that can be branded.[33] The problem is that many people want the brand image of integrity while still being able to engage in their own work in the ways they desire; Denton Marks refers to these people as "free riders" who, if allowed to proliferate, can destroy the very brand from which they derive benefits.[34] So, how can we build brand equity, that is, loyalty to academic integrity, awareness of academic integrity, and perceived quality of academic integrity?[35]

J. Douglas Toma, a higher education researcher at the University of Georgia, and co-authors suggest that brand equity can be developed in several ways. One may be by identifying "benchmarks relative to competitors."[36] To elaborate on this strategy, it might be helpful to turn to other successful education brands such as internationalization, sustainability, or diversity. Educational institutions are able to claim these brands by measuring their benchmarks through systems or "scorecards"[37] provided by external agencies. For example, the Association for the Advancement of Sustainability in Higher Education (AASHE), which only began in 2005, offers a Sustainability Tracking, Assessment, and Rating System (STARS) which is a "voluntary, self-reporting framework for gauging relative progress toward sustainability for colleges and universities."[38] There is no similar benchmark tool that is available for gauging progress toward academic integrity culture creation, though Drinan and Bertram Gallant have published a first step toward that with their institutionalization survey.[39] Educational institutions could, perhaps, brand themselves as "integrous" once they achieve a certain level of institutionalization (see next section on academic integrity institutionalization for more information).

Brand equity can also be developed when institutions have clear "norms, values, and beliefs that they continually announce and reinforce through symbols, language, narratives, and practices."[40] In the academic integrity and CharacterCounts! literature, schools are encouraged to develop brand equity around integrity by instituting symbols and rituals such as an honor code, an honor code signing ceremony, an honor pledge that students write and sign on each assignment, and so on. However, to build equity on the integrity "brand," and to motivate students to choose integrity over dishonesty, we argue that the target of those symbols cannot be restricted to the student population. There should be equal attention paid to integrity in the work of teachers, researchers, staff, and administrators.

There should be congruency between the school's rhetoric and its actions, and when there is not, the fixes should be public and openly discussed by school leaders. For example, teachers or administrators who alter grades or plagiarize should receive sanctions similar to those that a student would receive (or perhaps more severe in recognition that adults "should know better"). Student athletes should not be given special privileges or easy grades. And, if the university boasts a quality undergraduate education, faculty should be provided with sufficient support and encouragement to engage in good teaching, not just good research. The ethical development of students can only be facilitated and encouraged toward integrity if the environment around them is structured for ethical behaviors and integrity is more than a "brand" but a representative of the actual institutional culture which has, "at its core . . . a clearly articulated and lived mission that captures the commitment of every person in the organization"[41] (see Table 6.2 for a summary of branding academic integrity).

Attending to the Ethical Conduct of Teachers

The moral judgment and action of our students should not be our only concern when considering long-term deterrents to student cheating. As we saw in Chapter 2, student cheating occurs in the midst of greater educational corruption by teachers and administrators. And,

Table 6.2 Strategies and questions to ask for branding academic integrity

---

√ Identify your school's integrity benchmarks against your competition. For example,

- Does your campus have an expressed commitment to academic integrity?
- Does your school have a policy and process for academic integrity?
- Is cheating regularly reported and sanctioned?

√ Highlight the academic integrity artifacts (e.g., symbols, language, practices) that represent academic integrity norms, values, and beliefs of the campus.

- Do your campus authorities model academic integrity by holding themselves to high ethical standards and demonstrating accountability for their actions?
- Does your campus predominantly display your integrity policy or honor code?
- Can students recite or explain your integrity or ethical statements and/or honor code?
- Can teachers and administrators also?
- Do students stop their peers from cheating and do they talk to teachers about academic integrity?

√ Enhance congruency between the school's rhetoric and actions and openly talk about it.
- Do teachers and administrators allow/overlook cheating that occurs?
- When teachers or administrators violate ethical principles, are they held accountable?
- Is your campus able to realize all of the promises it makes (e.g., a high quality undergraduate education, fairness), or otherwise address them with a high level of transparency and accountability?
- Do teachers and administrators plagiarize other school's materials (e.g., strategic plans, mission statements, vision statements, etc.) but expect students not to plagiarize?

---

as Kibler argued, "failure to insist that faculty members demand high ethical standards communicates a mixed message to students and creates an environment not conducive" to academic integrity.[42]

In the News

Students do not cheat alone. In several states across the country, investigations have uncovered teachers and administrators who have helped students cheat in order to raise the school's test scores. These investigations have found that teachers "read off answers during a test, [let] students . . . correct wrong answers," prep students on questions from upcoming standardized tests, use signals during the test to guide students to the correct answers, calculate "math problems while [students take] the mandatory state test" and "alter [sic] student tests."

From *The Associated Press* (2003, October 28), "Teachers caught cheating: Some critics blame pressure of standardized testing," by Michael Gormley. Retrieved December 11, 2008, from www.cbsnews.com/stories/2003/10/28/national/main580355.shtml

---

Faculty and teacher moral development can be a sensitive area to explore. On the one hand, their relatively high status and image as role models make them crucial to any movement to strengthen academic integrity and education. They are "on the line" with students in intensive interactions. On the other hand, their very closeness to students may lead them to "not harm" a student who has cheated. As we saw earlier in Chapter 4, teachers may ignore cheating because they do not want to embarrass a student or get mired in administrative or legal hassles. Or, they may just not want to believe that their students cheat.

Teachers are not perfect, of course, and so we should not expect perfection of them. What we should expect is professionalism and ethical conduct. However, to expect it, we should know if and how faculty, high school teachers, and college professors learn professional ethics, that is, their obligations and responsibilities to each other, their students, and society. It is fairly clear to most that toleration of student academic dishonesty constitutes ethical failure on the part of teachers, and we have heard some of their reasons for ignoring it. But, these reasons may be no more illuminating on the problem than students' own neutralizations of their ethical failures (the cheating itself). To really understand why faculty ignore cheating, we need to look at the contours of the academic profession.

John Bruhn and his colleagues, who wrote a piece on the ethical failings of higher education faculty, argue that "there are no universally recognized set of standards defining appropriate and inappropriate conduct on the part of faculty."[43] Most professions have codes of conduct or ethics policies to guide the behaviors of membership – consider those in place for engineers, doctors, and accountants, for example. Why is there not a similar code for the profession of teaching that transcends organizational boundaries?[44] Part of the answer is a focus on rights, mainly the professor's right to academic freedom and individual autonomy. Ironically, perhaps, the language of rights is far more dominant and powerful than the language of duties or obligations when speaking of the teaching profession. This focus on rights is easily reinforced by the structure of the profession itself – the world of teachers and faculty members is often an isolated one, that is, a teacher has his classroom under his direct supervision, and much of his work (for example, grading papers, conducting research, writing) is done solitarily and in private.

Of course, the independence of faculty does have limits. A mathematics teacher who talks about politics all semester would not be seen as competent. Neither would a chemistry teacher who used unsafe laboratory experiments. But faculty are given great flexibility in choosing teaching techniques, and they are expected to both motivate students and police their classroom conduct. It is not easy for an individual to play both good cop and bad cop, and faculty are expected to use their judgment about which student behaviors they will police most strongly. Most faculty understand the necessity of intervening when student behaviors disrupt teaching or create a hostile learning environment, but there is less agreement on the necessity of stopping student cheating, which is often done quietly and secretively with little overt impact on classroom dynamics. Faculty can deny that cheating is occurring, downplay the negative effects that cheating can have on the larger class, and neutralize their responsibility to interfere with a student who is "just hurting himself."

In the News

"Universities in the Croatian capital of Zagreb were raided today by police officers investigating professors who were suspected of taking bribes for awarding inflated grades or securing spots for students in oversubscribed courses."

From *The Chronicle of Higher Education* (2008, September 18), "Croatian universities raided by police in pursuit of bribe-taking professors," by Aisha Labi. Retrieved September 18, 2008, from www.chronicle.com

---

However, society does have high standards for teachers, and Bruhn and colleagues looked to how citizenship, professionalism, and institutions get linked in these expectations. A teacher is not stranded on a desert island, but exists and performs within a profession and an institution. Bruhn and his colleagues do distinguish "individual failure" from "organizational failure" but admit that there are "gray areas" between them.[45] We argue that failure to confront student academic dishonesty exists in this zone and has incredibly serious consequences for both moral development and institutions. Teachers may see the ethical failure of student cheating but not their own ethical failure of not confronting it. Compounding this may be that most teachers do not see student cheating as serious nor do they see the contagious qualities of cheating. One can condemn the individual teacher but teachers learn about citizenship and professionalism in institutions. Thus, it is the responsibility of institutions, with faculty and administrators working together, to develop and articulate the ethical responsibilities and professional obligations of teachers. Most academic integrity policies "require" faculty to report student cheating, but often these requirements are not followed up upon or enforced. Institutions need to find a way to connect faculty to their duty to report and to enhance academic integrity; this takes us back to an earlier argument to reward and brand academic integrity, but it also takes us forward to the next long-term deterrent: institutionalization of academic integrity.

Institutionalizing Academic Integrity: Toward a New Conceptualization

In a previously published piece in the *Canadian Journal of Higher Education*, Bertram Gallant and Drinan wrote that the research on academic integrity has led to a consensus on "five logically related propositions":

1. The incidence of student cheating and plagiarism is consistently high on our campuses and is deeply worrisome.
2. Student-run honour code systems have measurably lower incidence of self-reported cheating than administratively or faculty-driven systems.
3. It is difficult to create and sustain a student-run honour code system, and there is little experience with them in most parts of the United States and virtually none in Canada.
4. It is feasible and desirable to provide for diffusion of best practices in deterring and managing student cheating and plagiarism.
5. A culture of integrity can be formed which minimizes cheating and has advantages for the whole of the academy.[46]

Encouraging best practices (such as those described in Chapter 5 and the moral development of students and teachers described earlier) are important, but the challenge is creating a culture of integrity which provides the signals that shape values and the structures that support ethical behavior. How do we see institutions doing this for academic integrity?

One could suppose that a step-by-step process of making incremental improvements should occur. But change does not occur in this fashion. Even biologists note that evolutionary changes can be abrupt, and it is essential to know where to begin. In the social sciences we can imagine where a process can end and then plan for it. To institutionalize academic integrity, we suggest that the process proceeds in recognizable stages. Educational organizations and their constituents and supporters should be able to identify what stage they are at and what needs to be done to move to another stage. A given campus should have a consensus on what stage characterizes the current situation.

New conceptualizations of the process of institutionalization are required, and these must be as straightforward and as elegant as possible so that all constituents – the public through students, faculty, and academic leaders – can understand, clearly communicate, and all get on the same page. We suggest four stages with the fourth stage being institutionalization of academic integrity. Notice that the fourth stage is not necessarily a student-run honor code. Rather, we conceptualize it as a point where student academic honesty is integrated into organizational routines, is a stable norm that guides teaching and research, and acts as a value that binds the community of the campus. Every school, not just student-run honor codes, can attempt to achieve this fourth stage. But where do we begin?

We call the first stage "recognition and commitment." In this stage, the educational organization must recognize that there is an issue and commit to addressing it. There must be discontent with the current situation and dialogue about it among faculty and academic administrators, at a minimum. Often this is triggered by a cheating scandal, when there is both a sense of urgency of dealing with the problem and a commitment to doing something about it. Occasionally "champions" come forward to keep the issue alive, but frequently a campus will lose momentum or other issues will come forward that will shift attention.

Hints that Your School is at Stage One

Are faculty bemoaning the amount of student cheating?

Are conversations or questions about academic integrity regularly popping up in campus meetings about other related issues (e.g., curriculum, student services, student conduct)?

Are students approaching faculty with complaints about cheating in class?

Are faculty asking for help with teaching or dealing with student cheating?

In her study of academic integrity institutionalization in three postsecondary education institutions, Bertram Gallant found that "discontent" can take many forms and need not be instigated by a dramatic cheating scandal.[47] Certainly, larger research universities may need a scandal to instigate action, but smaller schools may only need one person who has a desire and the time to encourage action. Of course, sometimes "scandals" are actually ignored by administrators who choose the interests of parents and children over the interests of the school. Piper High School in Kansas provides one such example; the teacher there quit after the school board overturned her decision to fail her students for plagiarizing. One parental or teacher champion, then, may not be sufficient if the faculty as a whole or the campus administrators are not interested in campus reform.

It is the flagging of momentum that can lead to simply staying at the first stage. In the worst case, the issue may disappear entirely from radar screens until the next outbreak of cheating is seen. But it is possible that the campus will begin to generate a response to the cheating problem. This can lead to the second stage, "response generation."

Response generation must be more than a short-term reaction to the issue; it needs to be methodical, that is, studying the problem in depth and structuring conversations about how to deal with the problem. These conversations must be candid, and skeptical voices must be heard. Teachers, for example, need to be able to express their frustrations and fears about the time and effort needed to confront student academic dishonesty. Stage Two is usually considered successful when people conclude that cheating is not simply a moral failure and an individual problem, but one that requires attention by the whole organization.

Typically, there are decisions to develop academic integrity policies and procedures in Stage Two or reinvigorate dormant and under-utilized policies and procedures. A coalition of teachers, students, and administrators will usually come together so that expectations on academic honesty can be articulated to incoming students and new teachers. But implementing even these modest initiatives can also lose momentum if resources are not mobilized and organizational routines changed. Stage Two does not automatically lead to Stage Three, implementation, and can actually regress to Stage One.

Hints that Your School is at Stage Two

Are faculty and students willing to come together to talk about the student cheating problem and generate solutions?

Has faculty senate offered to revisit the school's academic honesty policy?

Do folks on campus want to know how much cheating is occurring and what students and faculty think about it?

Are there groups who are already working on generating solutions to the problem?

Has someone volunteered to take the lead on an academic integrity initiative?

Stage Three, implementation, occurs when the technical core of the educational organization, particularly teachers and principals/deans, have integrated academic integrity innovations into standard operating procedures. Teachers need to know *exactly* what they need to do in confronting cheating and have confidence that administrators will support them. Students are regularly informed about academic integrity policies and procedures and have clarity about when collaboration, and how much, is permitted on projects. Here, too, momentum may flag, and it is possible that campus will fall back into Stage One or Two. It is almost impossible, however, for the academic integrity issue to fall back to Stage One once achieving Stage Three.

Hints that Your School is at Stage Three

Is there a clear academic integrity policy that people understand and is readily available?

Are the procedures for reporting student cheating known, followed, and fair?

Is "academic integrity" a regularly spoken phrase on campus?

Does campus leadership speak publically to academic integrity and reinforce its importance to the overall campus mission?

Are there structures and resources to support the policy and the academic integrity initiative?

The fourth stage, institutionalization, moves implementation forward so it is fully integrated into campus life. Some cheating will still occur, but the campus community knows how to deal with it and expectations for integrity are widely held and consistently displayed and propagated. The holy grail of academic integrity for many schools has been the creation of a student-run honor code. Students in such schools typically report half the cheating rates of nonhonor-code schools. Of course, we do not know for certain if students in honor-code schools cheat less, or are simply less willing to admit that they are cheating. Tapping the idealism of students seems so promising yet very few schools can succeed at creating student-run honor codes because it is a difficult and long process. The realization of this can be crushing to young people.

Hints that Your School is at Stage Four

Do new students and faculty cite a culture of academic integrity as a reason for wanting to be a part of the campus?

Is the academic integrity and academic ethical culture routinely audited to pinpoint and rectify problems and obstacles?

Are teachers and students regularly rewarded for academic integrity and ethical conduct?

Can faculty trust students to complete academic assignments in the intended ways without significant proctoring?

Do campus members routinely consider the ethical implications of an action or decision before other factors (such as monetary or reputational)?

Are conversations about academic integrity and ethics an ongoing and ingrained part of the campus culture?

At this point, we must confront the notion that a student-run honor code is the epitome of the fourth stage. It is certainly desirable in most people's minds, and student idealism often grabs for the golden ring of a student-run honor code. The best may be the enemy of the good, though, and it is useful to think about honor codes as representing qualities also shown by other successful manifestations of academic integrity (even a school with an honor code may not be at Stage

Four if the idea of "honor" exists only on paper). Debates on a given campus about academic integrity can get bogged down by how to create student-run honor codes that work. Often this usefully leads to experiments with modified honor codes in which there is collaboration among students, faculty, and academic administrators in making institutionalization work. It is in this crucible, rather than in a fully student-run honor code, that we should look for new conceptualizations of how to institutionalize academic integrity. And the beauty of this new conceptualization is that it can apply to all levels of education from elementary to graduate schools.

The Dynamic Nature of Institutionalization

It is possible to slip back into a previous stage even if the campus made it to Stage Four (see Figure 6.1 for the messiness of the institutionalization process). Policies and procedures may atrophy or a new generation of students and faculty may not be properly socialized into the academic integrity system. Consistency and reliability of leadership on campuses are required. A consciousness that there could be slippage to an earlier stage is tremendously important to the ability to stay on any stage but is particularly important in Stage Four.

This four-stage model of institutionalization of academic integrity is easy to understand and can help champions of academic integrity plan to move from one stage to the next. It is also useful for its realism as it accepts the notion of slippage from one stage to a previous one. Idealism about promoting change needs to be tempered by

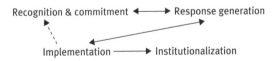

Figure 6.1 The messiness of the institutionalization process

the reality that slips can occur. One should keep attention on not only getting to the next stage but also staying on a given stage if momentum or circumstances change.

One of the greatest values of this four-stage model of institution-alization of integrity is that it relies on common understanding of where a campus is. While there may be legitimate disagreements about what stage a campus is located at during times of transition, it typic-ally should be *easy* to forge consensus about which stage you are on. This will help an educational organization be strategic about plans to move forward or to prevent slippage to an earlier stage. Agreeing on what stage a campus is on during self-studies for accreditation is important. And simply "singing from the same page" is important so that discourse about student cheating can be profitable. It ought to be possible for a parent to show a principal the chart of the four stages and have that person give the same answer as a teacher in the school or even a student about what stage the school is at.

Campuses that reach Stage Four may be able to "brand" themselves as an "integrity school," yet, in the absence of an objective certifi-cation, it may be exceptionally difficult to brand integrity as an identity marker. The most likely trajectory is that an association, such as the CAI, could become that certifying association. But it could be a slow process for a school to move through the four stages and gain external validation of its achievement.

While Stage Four may be the most desirable as a goal, it is more important to have agreement on which stage a school is at. Any stage can be worthwhile and pretending to be at a stage where one is not is unhelpful – indeed may be dishonest – in moving forward on academic integrity. It may not even be important that we seek to get every school to Stage Four; Stage Three itself is a viable one and can advance academic integrity, especially if we proliferate the number of schools that are at Stage Three. Unfortunately, many campuses are not even at Stage One, and the academic integrity movement will not be seen as succeeding until most campuses are on Stages One through Three.

Conclusions

As we saw earlier in the book, behaviors defined by the educational institution as academic cheating are not always viewed by students as morally reprehensible – some view the behaviors as merely morally disagreeable. Let's revisit our driving illustration provided in the first chapter. If we gathered ten people, each at the same moral development stage, some may see speeding as a moral problem while others see it as merely "disagreeable." However, it is likely if we add even one variable to the hypothetical to suggest that a driver killed a pedestrian because he was speeding, the "do no harm" value would be invoked and there might be more agreement on the moral reprehensibility of the act.

This means that teaching students or developing in them the ability to make moral judgments, establish moral intent, and then engage in moral behavior will not be an effective long-term deterrent by itself. Rather, changing social conceptions of various academic behaviors from merely disagreeable to morally reprehensible is critical. The academic institution is in the best position to do this because "the general intellectual milieu of colleges and universities . . . fosters the exchange of ideas, exposure to multiple perspectives regarding social issues, academic values of truth-seeking and careful reasoning, [and] institutional values of academic integrity and personal responsibility."[48] However, to do this, schools and colleges must be willing to tackle the problem in ways that are deep, profound, and transformative.

As the issue of student academic dishonesty gains public attention, token efforts to deal with it will be perceived as such. Sexual misconduct in the professions has seen a similar curve. Education would be better served by confronting the issue now, particularly since many of the tools are available. But the reasons to act now fundamentally come down to two: (1) the threat is to the essential mission of education, teaching and learning; and (2) student academic dishonesty is pervasive, far more pervasive than the other issues of corruption in education that come to public attention.

We end this chapter with a conversation between a college president and a professor that captures the critical need and timeliness of developing a long-term deterrent to student cheating. The next chapter will explore how we – as citizens, educators – can make academic honesty more central to the educational agenda and begin to move more schools through the stages of institutionalization of academic integrity. We will also explore the practical ways we can accelerate specific best practices for dealing with the problem of student academic dishonesty. And we will display examples of key conversations of students, teachers, and the public about moral development that go considerably beyond the "teaching moments" when students are caught in an act of academic dishonesty.

PROFESSOR: You know it is going to take a long time to gear up the college to confront student cheating, and most presidents serve under six years.

PRESIDENT: Agreed, but it is getting to be an issue we cannot ignore, and even accreditation agencies are putting pressures on us.

PROFESSOR: It is such a big issue – how do they expect us to solve it when student cheating has been around forever and the students come to college already experienced in cheating their way through school. Besides, we are college faculty who specialize in particular disciplines; we can't be "moral caretakers" for our thousands of students.

PRESIDENT: On the contrary. We are always teaching them what is acceptable behavior and what is not – just by what we say and do! Even if values are "caught" rather than taught, we have them with us for four years and hopefully decades as alums, so we should be able to make an impact!

PROFESSOR: Okay, but I still do not see how we can gear up for this – you're going to get push-back from faculty who already feel overworked and overstressed because of the increasing demands being made on us to publish, publish, publish! And, I've heard that professors who have reported student cheating end up spending too much time in court fighting with the student and, perhaps even worse, with negative student evaluations which their department chairs hold against them! How can you expect faculty to get on board when they feel like they are punished for trying to create classrooms of integrity?

PRESIDENT: You've made some really great points. We definitely have to work on supporting our faculty better. I think we start with a realistic goal – making cheating clearly unacceptable even if the rate does not go down much. Just as we have a master plan for facilities and a strategic plan for internationalizing the curriculum, we can have one on institutionalizing academic integrity. We need everyone on board – students, faculty, administrators and my cabinet – and we need to tackle the challenges that each of those groups feels in upholding a culture of integrity on our campus.

Table 6.3 Guidelines for advancing the institutionalization of academic integrity

---

STAGE 1: Building **recognition** of, and **commitment** to addressing, the problem of academic dishonesty

Conduct institutional self-assessment to get folks on same page re: the stage your campus is at.[1]

Complete the Center for Academic Integrity Assessment Guide to assess the academic integrity climate on campus (focusing on student and faculty)

At the high school level, talk to parents about academic integrity and cheating to assess their perceptions and attitudes

Create a representative coalition to guide institutional actions (in high school, this coalition should include parents, students, teachers, and administrators; in college, this coalition should be led by faculty and include teachers and administrators)

Principal/president should speak publically about the problem and openly commit the institution to addressing it

Governing boards should publically express support for the initiative and, where possible, provide the resources that will be necessary

Table 6.3 *(cont'd)*

STAGE 2: **Generating** institutional **responses** to the problem

Review the results of the CAI assessment to pinpoint problem areas (for example, specific behaviors that are most prevalent, reasons students give for cheating, reasons faculty give for not reporting)

Review existing policies and procedures that support or inhibit an ethical culture. For example, do tenure and promotion policies hurt faculty who report cheating? Is there an existing academic integrity policy that is unworkable? Are the current procedures cumbersome?

Rework existing policies and procedures or craft new ones

Revisit the institution's strategic plan and determine how academic integrity fits in

Craft an academic integrity curriculum – e.g., orientations, seminars, and text for faculty to use and adapt

Conduct focus groups with key campus constituencies to unearth more in-depth information than provided by surveys already conducted

STAGE 3: **Implementing** the generated solutions and responses

Create institutional manuals/guides, for preventing, detecting, and responding to cheating

Hire staff and open offices to support the responses generated by the coalition and larger campus

Recruit students to act as academic integrity peer educators

Recruit faculty to act as academic integrity advisors and advocates within their departments

Ensure ongoing fiscal and rhetorical support from the principal/president/boards for the academic integrity initiative

Include academic integrity in core institutional documents – mission statement, admissions material, websites

Host regular dialogues about academic integrity and cheating

STAGE 4: Achieving and sustaining the **institutionalization** of academic integrity

Assess the academic integrity climate at least every two–three years

Ask for an external review by the Center for Academic Integrity or Transparency International

Continually monitor and update policies and procedures as needed

---

[1] Drinan & Bertram Gallant, 2008.

Chapter 7

The Call for Action and Wisdom

Conversations that Make a Difference

"When we humans don't talk to one another, we stop acting intelligently. We give up the capacity to think about what's going on. We don't act to change anything . . . It takes courage to start a conversation. But if we don't start talking to one another, nothing will change. Conversation is the way we discover how to transform our world, together."[1]

In this volume we have confirmed the severity of the problem of student academic misconduct, explored its nature, and sketched out how to deal with it. In our final chapters we pull together practical suggestions to move education through each stage of improvement in dealing with the problem of student cheating. This will constitute a call to action to the public and educators, a call to action that cannot be postponed. When the elephant in the room is pointed out to people – and they admit seeing it – you cannot continue to ignore it even if you debate what to do about it.

Institutionalizing integrity is desirable even as it is difficult and long term. It takes educational leaders of courage to make this happen, and it needs clear support from parents and the public. The call to action must have at its core the revival of teaching and learning as the essential missions of education. The teacher–student relationship is key to progress. The point is not to condemn teachers for avoiding the necessity to confront. Rather, it is in supporting and rewarding them for recommitting themselves to the progressive idealism in reaching young people and making a difference to them. Committed educators know that they make a difference to their students not only in key skills, but in their character or moral development. We need to proliferate these moral conversations not only among educators and students, but also among parents and the public. Instigating these conversations is the purpose of this book, especially since these conversations need to take place *before* a cheating scandal overwhelms a school, teacher, or students and their parents. Confronting cheating cannot only be about using a given incident as a "teachable moment." These teachable moments are important, but we argue that *sustained* conversations are required to strengthen our academic institutions.

Margaret Wheatley, world-renowned author and leadership expert, wrote a treatise on the power of conversation to change the world and solve the problems that continue to confront societies. In her book, she argues that humans have always come together to solve problems, regardless of cultural background or place in time; "human conversation is the most ancient and easiest way to cultivate the conditions for change – personal change, community and organizational change, planetary change."[2] So, before we return to the practicalities of teachable moments, we will first explore the kinds of conversations that teachers, parents, administrators, and the public could usefully proliferate in order to reduce student cheating and create cultures of academic integrity in our schools and on our higher education campuses. Two different kinds of conversations (A and B) are showcased to illustrate the differences between dialogues that neutralize action and change, and those that incite it.

Teacher-to-Teacher

Conversation A

TEACHER ONE: I am a compassionate person – why should I penalize a student and complicate my life by turning in a student for cheating in my course?

TEACHER TWO: How is compassion going to help that student grow? And others will surely know about it. This could get out of hand.

TEACHER ONE: I should just have a word privately with the student to tell him I know and that there will be a severe penalty next time.

TEACHER TWO: So he'll be more careful?

TEACHER ONE: That's not the point! What good can come with turning him into the principal – it will just get ugly, and I'll have to spend valuable time defending myself and filling out paperwork and worrying about being sued by a parent. Give me a break!

Conversation B

TEACHER ONE: I am a compassionate person – why should I penalize a student and complicate my life by turning in a student for cheating in my course?

TEACHER TWO: I used to think that way but you know that the principal's office is well equipped to handle this. You do not want your professional reputation tarnished by ignoring cheating.

TEACHER ONE: I am not going to ignore it – I am going to talk to the student one-on-one – he'll get the message.

TEACHER TWO: But how about the rest of the class? You can't violate student privacy by making a scene in front of the class.

TEACHER ONE: I would not make a scene – they'll just know how angry and disappointed I am. That should send the message.

169

TEACHER TWO: You've seen the statistics on cheating – students know how much cheating is going on – they'll just think that one student was unlucky.

TEACHER ONE: Well, it's my business and I'll do what I want.

TEACHER TWO: Your chat with me now tells me something else and the whole school has been alerted to how to handle this properly – you know that.

School President-to-Governing Board Member (GBM)

Conversation A

GBM: I've read another article on cheating in schools. How do we measure up – what are we doing about it?

PRESIDENT: Our student affairs office worries about it because they have jurisdiction over most discipline issues, but unfortunately faculty control cheating and plagiarism – and they don't have a handle on it yet.

GBM: Well, if students and student affairs staff seem willing to tackle it, why not just tell them to develop a student-run honor code?

PRESIDENT: I wish it were that easy – it will take much effort and time. This current crop of students is eager, but most of them graduate next year.

GBM: You can lead the faculty, then, can't you? You were so good two years ago in getting them to internationalize the curriculum.

PRESIDENT: That was different – everyone knew about globalization and the need for global literacy.

GBM: As I recall, it wasn't that easy – you had some entrenched faculty interests, and many faculty saw internationalization as elitist and a current fad.

PRESIDENT: I was able to get it done because of a dedicated group of faculty champions who are respected. Cheating is different – it embarrasses faculty when it happens – they get outraged but the emotion does not last that long.

GBM: They know it is going on then?

PRESIDENT: Sure – and they take some measures against it – but it is just not on their collective radar screen.

GBM: So, where does that leave us?

Conversation B

GBM: I've read another article on cheating in schools. How do we measure up – what are we doing about it?

PRESIDENT: We are like most schools – a persistent set of problems on this score. We recently completed a survey of our students, and it even shocked faculty when they saw the statistics.

GBM: Well, it should have shocked the students, too. Can we see the stats at our next governing board meeting?

PRESIDENT: No problem – your support in addressing the issue will be helpful to me because I can no longer let this issue simmer. Even the accreditation agencies are getting fussy about it.

GBM: Well, how long before we see this turned around?

PRESIDENT: It is not as easy as you would think. I've got to arrange a coordinated approach on campus and lean on people – there is no magic wand, and sending it off to a committee for study will just lead to inaction.

GBM: What if you convened an all-day meeting of board members, key faculty, and student leaders to probe the problem and show how serious we are on the board to address it?

PRESIDENT: That will work, but I'll need to have a few months to set it up right so momentum will flow from it.

GBM: Great! Maybe we can help on the momentum side by giving faculty and students integrity awards – cash – each year.

PRESIDENT: That can be a piece of it – a new national association has formed to certify progress on academic integrity at schools – that should help, too, particularly if I insist that a section on academic integrity be included in all our self-studies for re-accreditation. Faculty take accreditation very seriously.

Principal-to-Parent of Teen Charged with Cheating

Conversation A

PARENT: My daughter did what most kids do. Your picking her out for punishment is patently unfair and will destroy her emotionally as she gets ready to take the SAT next week.

PRINCIPAL: We have our rules, and students have been warned.

PARENT: Well, we'll take it to the superintendent – you can't just smash up student lives, you know.

PRINCIPAL: I hear you on that – maybe we can find another way through this, but I don't know.

PARENT: I've heard you make exceptions – my kid is a good kid, not one of those troublemakers.

PRINCIPAL: True – let me think about this, talk to the teacher, and see if we have some wiggle room.

PARENT: Good. I'd hate to bother my lawyer on this trivial stuff.

Conversation B

PARENT: My daughter did what most kids do. Your picking her out for punishment is patently unfair and will destroy her emotionally as she gets ready to take the SAT next week.

PRINCIPAL: We thought about that, and she and the counselor are working out a way to handle this and postpone the SAT exam for her for a couple of weeks. We have experience dealing with this.

PARENT: Still, other kids are getting away with it and my daughter denies it was cheating anyway. I believe her.

PRINCIPAL: We believe in your daughter, too. She is turning into a fine young woman, and we are careful on these things. This is her first offense, and so she's getting a warning and an 'F' grade on that exam – she still can do well in the class. If she cheats again, she'll be in deep trouble.

> But our experience is that students shape up really well after a warning and a note in their file. That is purged at graduation, as you know, if there are no other cheating incidents.

PARENT: I'm still very unhappy with all of this – what can I do?

PRINCIPAL: It's frustrating for all of us. But if we let it go, it will tarnish our reputation. Love your daughter and support her – there are far worse things that can happen to young people. But also talk to her about cheating and why it is wrong to take short cuts to get ahead or to cheat because "everyone else is doing it." Perhaps you and your daughter can help correct the situation by talking to other parents and students about cheating?

The difference between conversations A and B in each case was one primarily of how well an institution was geared up to handle problems of student academic dishonesty. Schools can rely on skillful faculty and staff to create teaching moments when students are caught cheating. But, as the above conversations show, this is often too little, too late. Schools need more systematic ways to monitor and regulate cheating than simply gaining the admission from a student who is engaged in cheating that their behavior was wrong. Teaching moments are not enough to sustain a strategy of institutionalizing academic integrity. But they can be very important and should not be neglected.

Teachable Moments *Are* Important

The following conversations illustrate how students, parents, teachers, and administrators can help students learn and grow developmentally from a cheating incident. To discuss teachable moments, we take one "cheating incident" involving student Sally and play out the conversations that surround that incident.

Instructor-to-Student

INSTRUCTOR: I'd like to talk to you about your paper. Are you satisfied with the outcome and the experience of writing the paper?

SALLY: Yeah. I think I did a really good job. I worked really hard on it and gave you all the content you asked for. So, I think it's an A paper.

INSTRUCTOR: Okay, but what was the process like? Can you tell me how you went about learning about the topic and writing the paper?

SALLY: Well, you know. I just did some research and then started writing. Nothing special. I don't know. What do you want me to say?

INSTRUCTOR: The reason I assign this paper is to facilitate your knowledge of the topic and your growth as a writer. One of the skills that employers and graduate schools look for is an ability to write coherently, clearly, and creatively – society needs better communicators all around so it's my hope and my job to help you develop those skills. Unfortunately, I am worried that you missed the opportunity to do that in this paper. As you know, your paper was checked with plagiarism detection software and it identified that 60 percent of your paper was copied from other sources.

SALLY: Well, obviously I read them! You told us we needed at least five outside sources in our paper so I did that! And I provided transition sentences before and after the stuff from other places – isn't that what you wanted?

INSTRUCTOR: Your simple copying of the other sources means that you may have not understood the sources you read and did not struggle with the difficult process of writing your own work based on your reading the work of other writers. This is how we construct knowledge – not simply by copying other folks' stuff. I'm going to have to give you an F on this paper and, unfortunately, report you to the academic integrity office for

plagiarism. That's school policy *and* I think it's important for your development as a writer because the
academic integrity office will enroll you in training
sessions to help you learn how to incorporate other
people's words and ideas and improve your writing.

SALLY: What?!?!? This is going to ruin my life. You can't do
this to me. Just give me an F – it's not fair to punish
me like this.

INSTRUCTOR: You were instructed in how to use sources, you knew
that your paper was going to be checked for copied
source material, and you did not seek out help from
myself or the teaching assistants in writing the paper.
You had several other alternative courses of action from
which you could choose, but you chose the wrong one.
And one thing that's important for you to learn is there
are consequences for every action we choose to take.

Student-to-Parent

SALLY: Mom, I am so mad right now! I have this horrible teacher
who can't teach, doesn't know what she's doing, and then
blames me for something that's really her fault!

MOM: Slow down. What has happened?

SALLY: I wrote this stupid paper using five external sources, just like
I was supposed to, and the freakin' professor doesn't like it,
says it's not good enough, and so is failing me and reporting me to some integrity office or something.

MOM: Hmmm. Integrity office? Sally, did you cite all of the sources
you used in your paper?

SALLY: I guess I might have missed some. But jeez – it's not like I
cheated on an exam or something! This is the same thing that
everyone does – we all copy and paste off the internet – but
she just decided to punish me. It's not fair!!

MOM: How did the professor know?

SALLY: We have to turn our papers in online and some computer
program checks our papers and then tells the professor
whether it's copied or not. Mine came up 60 percent!

175

MOM: Well, that sounds like the professor probably sees all the papers in the same way she sees yours then. What happens now?

SALLY: I get an F on the paper and I have to go to the academic integrity office and take some class or something on writing. I also have to go talk to my dean – I think this might go on my record! Mom – you have to do something about this. Can't you call our lawyer? They are going to rob me of my chance to go to law school!

MOM: Sally, I hear that you are really upset and I am so sorry that you are going through this right now. I will support you through this, but I'm not calling our lawyer. It sounds to me like you did something you were not supposed to do, they "caught" you fair and square, and now there's a policy and process for dealing with this. My advice is that you follow all of the steps you are supposed to, and maybe it won't be as bad as you think. You can call me anytime for advice or support, and please keep me in the loop about what's going on. I love you.

Student-to-Student Affairs Administrator (SAA)

SAA: So, Sally, it seems that you have had some trouble in one of your classes with an essay assignment?

SALLY: Yeah. I'm kind of still mad at the teacher but I talked with my mom and she said that I should follow the process and come talk to you about it. Am I in really big trouble?

SAA: Well, you might perceive it that way, I suppose. However, this is your first academic integrity policy violation so it could be worse, but there will be consequences that you will have to live with for a while.

SALLY: Like what?

SAA: Okay, so your professor turned in a packet of documents that show you plagiarized 60 percent of your essay.

SALLY: Plagiarism!!! Is that what she's calling this? I'm not a plagiarist – I just didn't cite some stuff very well!

SAA: Sally, the professor isn't calling it plagiarism – the university policy does. Plagiarism means using the words and ideas of others without attributing those words and ideas to that person. It is not a condemnation of your character, but it is a condemnation of your action. This university takes plagiarism very seriously because the essence of what we are and what we do – teaching, learning, and the construction of knowledge – is undermined by plagiarism.

SALLY: What's going to happen to me?

SAA: This is your first policy violation, so it will go on your record and if you violate the policy a second time, you could get suspended from the university. Sometimes we suspend students the first time for this much plagiarism, but the professor is convinced that your learning would be better served by enrolling you in some special writing classes to help you improve your skills and confidence as a writer. We really do not think that you were attempting to deceive the professor given that you knew your paper would be checked for plagiarism, so this seems to be a result of other issues. Besides struggling with writing, do you have some other things going on that you want to talk about?

SALLY: I don't know. Just the normal stuff, I guess. I'm trying to get used to university and the level of writing and work expected – it's much harder than high school! I also don't like the large classes – the professor said that I could have asked her or the teaching assistants for help, but I really didn't feel comfortable. They seem overworked and busy themselves – I felt bad bothering them. Besides, I didn't even realize that I needed their help or that they could help. I thought I had to struggle through this alone. The professor said so many times, "Do not work with others on this assignment. This is to be your own work in your own words!" I was scared to talk to anyone about the paper and then get accused of cheating, and now I am anyway!!!

SAA: You did make some poor decisions, but you can learn from this and become a better student in the long run. No one thinks anything less of you – we're here to support your growth and development as a person and a scholar, so take advantage of it. When you're out of school, you don't get too many second chances or this level of support when you mess up, so don't squander away this opportunity.

SALLY: Will this ruin my chances to get into law school?

SAA: It doesn't have to. You will have to tell law school that you were disciplined for academic misconduct, but in your application letter, you can reflect on the experience and what you learned and talk about how experiencing the process made you a better student and will make you a better lawyer! Institutions and people don't mind it when others make mistakes, but they hate it when people don't acknowledge their mistakes or when they don't learn or grow from them.

Student Affairs Administrator-to-Chief Academic Officer (CAO)

SAA: Hi, John. I'd like to talk to you about a major issue I think we have to resolve at the college – it has to do with developing students as writers and helping them grow and develop through ethical challenges. I just met with another student who was caught plagiarizing.

CAO: Oh, not this again. You know how the faculty feel – students should come to college prepared for writing, understanding about plagiarism, and already morally developed. Faculty do not believe that we should have to do what the lower education systems never managed to; if students can't hack it, they shouldn't be here.

SAA: John, this kid copied and pasted material into her paper even though she knew that the paper was being run through plagiarism detection software. Clearly she either does not understand how to incorporate others' words and ideas into her own work or she doesn't think that her professors will care; either way, that's a problem in my books.

CAO: Well, kick her out of school then. She can come back when she's ready to act like a grown-up and when she can write at the college level.

SAA: I didn't kick her out; even the professor thought she wouldn't be helped by that. We're going to get her into some intensive writing assistance. But you know what would really help? If we did more for and with students before this type of thing happened . . . Maybe our methods of assessing student readiness for college level work are not sufficient – high GPAs and SAT scores do not seem to cut it.

CAO: What do you suggest?

SAA: I think all first-year students should be enrolled in a first-year seminar that helps to socialize them into the culture of the academy and, at the same time, has them do some writing that can be assessed for identification of problem areas and level.

CAO: Some faculty have asked about that type of thing.

SAA: And I think we need a university-wide writing center. This student did not feel that she had anywhere to go for help – she didn't feel she could reach out to her instructor or teaching assistants and was told she had to do the paper independently, so didn't want to ask her parents or friends. But, if there was a writing center on campus, that might have been something she could have benefited from.

CAO: What about moral education – does she know she did a bad thing?

SAA: I think that, in this case, writing was a bigger issue but, yes, I think she's beginning to understand that she was facing an ethical dilemma and she made the wrong choice. I think that we can help move students along in ethical reasoning skills as well. What do you think? Can you help move faculty along with this idea? Is there funding for a writing center?

CAO: Let's start the discussion with faculty anyway – maybe we can use this as a teachable moment not just for the students, but for everyone on campus. We can't keep doing things the same way we've always done them, can we?

We hope the preceding conversation thread demonstrates that there are teachable moments for everyone in curbing the corruption that can stem from student cheating. We set the conversation on the college campus in this case, but the same conversation could happen in high schools and even elementary schools around the world. Within any level of education, the goal is to educate and to create a better future; while sometimes this may mean that a student has to be forced to take a break from formal education (through suspension), at other times it may mean that we have to seize upon the teachable moment that a student's (or teacher's, or administrator's, or parent's) mistake has offered us.

Sally's teacher did not condemn her and call her a cheater, but offered her a context for understanding why copying and pasting material is not acceptable. Sally's mom did not try to defend her daughter and attack the educational institution or teacher, but attempted to support Sally through the process of experiencing the consequences of her choices. The student affairs administrator acted as a guide for this learning and also attempted to leverage this incident as a moment to change the chief academic officer's mind about the solution to the plagiarism problem on campus.

The Moral Implications of Intellectual Growth: The Glass Half Full

We all know about "teachable moments." This book has demonstrated that those moments do not apply simply to students. Educators and parents need to initiate those moments and sustain them in prolonged conversations. The wisdom of students is apparent, especially when they point out how powerful it is for teachers (and parents) to speak frequently about the importance of integrity. We also have seen how concern for academic integrity has become a neutral port in the values wars, thus encouraging the development of a consensus moral vocabulary around values in education.

We have likewise noted how the business of education contributes to the analytical tools required to build academic integrity. This should not surprise us given the discussions of the relationships between economic and moral growth. Benjamin M. Friedman, in *The Moral Consequences of Economic Growth*, summarized the relationships of an "integrated view of scientific, economic, and moral progress" that have shaped the understandings and debates about economic growth over the last two centuries.[3] Ultimately, academic integrity is both embedded in these understandings and debates and also parallels it.

On Campus

Students of an academic integrity seminar were asked why there is such disparity between their accounts of their own academic conduct and that of their peers (the majority of students claim they don't cheat but those same students think that the majority of their peers do cheat). One student replied, "Maybe it's because after an examination, all you hear are stories about students cheating? No one ever comes out of an exam and says – that exam was so hard but I didn't cheat! I tackled it, struggled through it and did my best!"

This was such an astute observation and it makes us wonder – could we change the conversations that students have on our campuses about their academics so that they are filling the glass rather than emptying it?

Economic growth has been possible because we have been able to integrate our *knowledge* of science, economics, and morality to form new ideas and foster progress and, in turn, economic progress has rewarded characteristics that parallel academic integrity such as "reliability, order, and discipline."[4] The values of academic integrity and honesty are then aligned with practical notions of moral progress in ways unanticipated when we think of such classical ideals such as "virtue" or the pursuit of "truth." Thus, rather than see commerce and business as undermining academic integrity, we could choose to see commerce and business as reinforcing academic integrity.

But we should also see that there are consequences to *intellectual* growth distinct from economic growth. Ernest Boyer, a giant in the area of higher education reform, has spoken of the transitions from information to knowledge and then to wisdom that are inherent in education.[5] While we have been preoccupied with the excitement

181

of the information explosion the last three decades and while we speak of knowledge-based economies, there remains a deep hunger to achieve wisdom. Our schools have succeeded on the dimensions of information and knowledge, but can they succeed in advancing the growth of wisdom?

The language of wisdom is often seen as anti-intellectual because it seems to be ambivalent about the information and knowledge explosions rather than building upon them. But wisdom does build upon them in three ways: encouraging reflection on them; instilling behaviors that advance them; and creating institutions where information, knowledge, and wisdom can all thrive and connect intellectual and moral progress. There are several ways to do this in our educational organizations: we argue that the pursuit of academic integrity provides the premier vehicle to achieve this.

For example, we can reflect on the impact that the information and knowledge explosions have had on students' understandings of academic integrity. We have already argued that technology is most likely changing the ways in which younger people view information (as communal property rather than private property) and knowledge (as collaboratively constructed rather than individually developed).[6] Wisdom gained from such reflection might suggest that a more effective way for addressing student cheating is to address their conceptions of knowledge and information, not as incorrect but as occupying a space between the past and the future where conflicting ideas and practices are going to collide. Reflection of this nature, if sustained, might construct an ironic wisdom that we cannot easily require academic integrity (if that means adopting beliefs that are not their own) from individuals. Benjamin Friedman points out that it may be more effective to demand "*refraining* from unwanted action" than requiring positive action.[7] Ultimately, successful academic integrity systems are, in part, built by restraining dishonesty, greed, and selfishness, and such restraint has to come from educational institutions, peer groups, and individual self-restraint. The glass starts to become more than half full when we admit it is half empty and pay attention to not taking more water from it.

The next wisdom step is instilling behaviors that begin the process of filling the glass. For example, schools and colleges can begin to recognize behaviors that epitomize academic integrity and reward students, teachers, and administrators for choosing the ethical course of action. Teachers can highlight and applaud the students who engage in their education with honesty and integrity, despite the grades they ultimately receive. Schools can also do a better job of teaching students about the connections between the knowledge economy and the necessity of attributing information and knowledge to individuals, rather than to communes; students could understand this much more if they were ever able to experience economic and moral growth from the advancement of their own ideas, but rarely are they afforded this opportunity. Employers and graduate schools could also encourage honesty and integrity by de-emphasizing grades and rewarding students who demonstrate strength of character and courage to resist cheating, as well as the development of individual ideas and creative and critical thinking. This book has identified many other possible approaches for instilling positive behaviors – the key is to provide multiple and coordinated approaches that restrain dishonesty and encourage integrity.

The next wisdom step is creating institutions where information, knowledge, and wisdom can all thrive and connect intellectual and moral progress. Just as commerce has thrived by the invention of specialized institutions for finance, marketing, and research and development, so too can education thrive by conceptualizing and creating an institution of academic integrity within the educational institution. Academic integrity as an institution needs to be as central to education as the specialization of accounting is to a business. Academic integrity requires standards, professionalism, professionals, and a status that says it can only be ignored with great peril. Academic integrity becomes the guarantor of the integrity of the institution of education itself.

Can we envision a future scenario in which academic integrity is more important than test scores, tuition revenue, winning sports teams, lucrative research grants or other such end-measures of success?

A Vision of Success

It seems that much of the discussion about student academic dishonesty is driven by the "glass half empty." The scandals over cheating are most frequently swept under the rug. And when scandals do get public attention, they don't seem to have much of a shelf life. There seems to be so much left to do, and the negative profile dominates. But what about the glass being half full? And what if we could see our way to adding more to the glass? We know there are success stories – young people transformed after a teaching moment or inspired by attending a Center for Academic Integrity meeting. We know that some schools have struggled mightily to set up an honor code run by students. Others have systematically improved the operation of academic integrity policies and procedures even though they do not aspire to a student-run honor code. It is in these latter instances that we can find inspiration. Our vision of success ultimately must be Stage Four of academic integrity institutionalization, but that vision will be unique to each campus. And we may have to declare success at Stage Three of institutionalization even as we continue to aspire to Stage Four.

But what could that vision of success look like? Imagine the following speech of a college president to a conference filled with fellow presidents and governing board members:

> Colleagues and distinguished guests, ladies and gentlemen. Education has had many challenges but look at how we have responded. The majority of our young people now go into higher education, the changing demographics of our society have been brought into her institutions, technological revolutions absorbed and accelerated. But we are anxious about our successes and are preoccupied with the business of education – constantly worried that the resources required for maintenance and advancement of our institutions will be found wanting. But let us be reminded about what got us to today – a commitment to educating our young people, motivating them by our passion for the truth, and inspiring our best and brightest to follow us on the paths of scholarship and teaching.

We know that our passion for truth inspires and sustains our scholarship. But why can't it inspire our teaching in the same ways? We often do not share with our students the names of those on whose intellectual shoulders we stand as we deliver lectures in our classes. We too often tolerate student academic dishonesty, and thus the pursuit of truth seems distant to the world of the classroom. Imagine if we changed this: if professors took the same care at quoting sources for their lectures as they do in their publications, imagine how that could combine with institution-wide systems of confronting student academic dishonesty. The message would be that the pursuit of truth is implacably at the center of both teaching *and* research. The resonance can be astounding, the teaching-research debate among faculty transformed, and the coherence of education affirmed. We can do better!

We need a new rhetorical framework for what could be a grand new conversation in higher education with effects that will trickle down to K-12 education. We also need the same at the K-12 level, perhaps with a trickle-up to higher education. At every level, principal and presidential leadership is essential to this effort. We should expect principals and presidents to call for action; and, if we do not, the public and educators should demand to know why.

Action is driven by vision and we propose that an academic integrity movement be driven by a vision of education as the pursuit of truth and the transcendence of the divide between learning and testing (at the K-12 level) and teaching and research (at the higher education level). The rejuvenation of the teaching and learning mission needs to be more tightly linked with the responsibility of educational institutions to evaluate student learning, certify student mastery, conduct research, and create knowledge. It is not about increasing angst of faculty who are being asked to improve teaching while being pressured for more activity in other areas (such as research and service). And, in higher education, it is not about dividing our research faculty from our teaching faculty. Higher education in America has thrived because of the combined missions of teaching and research, a synergy that has made it the envy and the model of the world.

To teachers and faculty we must say: "Share your scholarship and sources more honestly and openly with students as you teach them and demand honesty from them in turn." This new social contract has many advantages: it increases the reciprocal obligations of both teachers and students; it commends the shared space in the pursuit of truth; and it connects scholarship and teaching in intimate ways that can be a broader model for other successful educational experiments.

What makes this vision viable and feasible is the leveling of the playing field of teachers and students on the matter of academic integrity. The issue of student academic integrity often seems to portray the failures of students as a problem to be confronted rather than as a bold challenge to education. By shaping the issue in its broader context, it moves the matter to positive territory rather than the arena of corruption. It moves academic dishonesty from an enforcement issue to a call for the rejuvenation of teaching and learning as a genuine and joint effort of teachers and students.

Back to the Future

There is one wisdom step left to recommend, and it can occur at any moment in the reflections on, and planning for, academic integrity: a candid self-examination of our own personal history with cheating in school. We are not urging confessions or public repudiation of past errors. We rather urge our readers to have a conversation with themselves, one that explores their personal experiences with an honesty about growth and character. We believe this conversation can deliver a very special empathy for those who cheat, those who don't, and those responsible for education in our society.

This conversation is needed even though our individual memories are almost certainly flawed.[8] But we have snippets of memories of cheating or not cheating in school that should be brought to the surface of our individual reflections. This honors the process of sustained reflection on confronting student cheating and provides perspective as we join the call for action. We can safely estimate that over 50 percent of the readers of this book cheated in school. We also know that, having read this far, you probably realize that we need, as individuals and as a society, to confront academic cheating. What kind of conversation with oneself can a person have? Below find three examples, but there are thousands possible given the idiosyncratic elements of all those experiences and our invariably selective memories.

Example 1: The Internal Conversation of One Who Did Not Cheat
"Why didn't I cheat in school? Was I afraid I'd get caught? Was I just lucky to have parents who nurtured me to virtuous habits? It's hard to know. I was really tempted that one time in high school when we had that pop quiz in math; my best friend sat right next to me, and he was ready for the quiz – I could have just peeked, but I didn't. It was a close call, though. What would've happened if I cheated then? I'm sure I would have gotten away with it. Would I've done it again, particularly since I did not like that teacher? Maybe. Maybe I was just lucky – who knows?"

Example 2: The Internal Conversation of an Occasional Cheater
"I had a terrible time in high school. All those hormones, and my folks were on their way to a divorce. I knew cheating was wrong but I hated life and was in revolt at both home and school. I cheated a couple of times early in college but had grown out of my rebellious stage. Why did I cheat less in college? It's hard to say. I guess I liked my major, and it seems like cheating was as much work as studying. That does not make me a great student, but I think I'm finally better off. Just how am I going to help my own kids not go down the same path?"

Example 3: The Internal Conversation of a Regular Cheater
"Okay – I cheated all the time in those business classes. I thought the business world was about cutting corners, and so I did. The profs didn't seem to care, and most of my fraternity thought it was cool to get away with it. Of course, we knew it was wrong, but at the time it

187

did not seem like a big deal. It's a big deal now – I have to trust my employees, and I can't worry about being screwed every time I cut a deal with my clients. Sometimes I wonder what would've happened if I had not cheated my way through the major. So I wish someone had caught me: Yeah, that one prof caught me plagiarizing, but she didn't really do anything about– just lectured me in her office. And that didn't stop me. And I wish I had not cut all those corners. I wonder how it could have all been different."

Our personal histories form a fabric of perspectives on not just cheating but also learning itself. We often learn more from our mistakes than when everything goes perfectly. Those responsible for learning, including each of us, know many of the obstacles to learning. Teaching is about removing obstacles to learning and reinforcing fundamental curiosities about how the world works. We often do not succeed because of the variety of ways learning occurs, unevenness in the pace of learning, or misunderstandings about how learning can happen. Student cheating is not only an obstacle to learning, of course, but unsophisticated ways in confronting it may also inhibit learning. Both teachers and students can gain from fresh and sustained efforts to take cheating seriously, and it may not be as difficult to accomplish as the magnitude of the problem suggests. In the next chapter, we show you how it can be done.

Chapter 8

Refining Our Tactics and Strategies

In order to think strategically, we must first decide the dimensions of an overall goal of the change we are aiming for as a social movement. Earlier, we established stages of institutionalization that tell us where we are in the process. How much change should we look for? There are four possibilities:

1. Crusading change
2. Challenging reform
3. Modest reform
4. Gestures or no change

Crusading change suggests that academic integrity should be the transforming and catalytic element in a wholesale reconstruction of the educational enterprise from elementary through graduate education. Crusading change assumes that the corruption of cheating is so insidious and is linked so closely to other flaws in how education is conducted that "back to the basics" must occur for the problem to be addressed. While the authors may have some sympathy with this revolutionary goal, the evidence has not shown that a dramatic increase in cheating has occurred nor that our institutions are so broken that they are bankrupt.

What seems to be evident is that students are not seeing cheating as morally reprehensible, especially in regard to homework, term papers, and other out-of-class assignments. And there has been progress in many parts of education in drawing attention to the problem of student cheating and finding ways to address it. One does not have to believe that student cheating is just symptomatic of a broader moral decay, thus justifying radical action. There are boundaries around academic integrity, meaning that targeted reforms can be effective. While confronting student cheating may raise conversations about other moral issues, it is a problem that is susceptible to management and some resolutions without undertaking a wholesale revolution of education. We explored these methods of managing cheating in earlier chapters.

On the other side, we obviously reject the "softness" of gestures or no change. Option 4 is not a call for action but rather inaction, or perhaps worse, a message of cynicism. The real choice is between options 2 and 3 – should we aspire to challenging reform or more modest reform? While readers and educators will have to make their own choice of goals, this volume is applying the rationale and components that can support either of the two goals. Most important is revisiting the stages of institutionalization established in Chapter 6. Those wanting change should be "on the same page" regarding where they are at in terms of institutionalization; a lack of clarity on this makes it very difficult to reach consensus on the ultimate goal.

We, of course, believe challenging reform is the best path to advance institutions to Stages Three and Four. Modest reforms can get a school through Stages One and Two and help schools stay at Stages Three and Four. But so few schools are at stages Three and Four that challenging reform is called for. We should be ambitious enough to aspire to Stages Three and Four and that requires courageous leadership and sustained, strategic action. It is *not* a time for modesty, but sometimes schools must start there to get experience with the issues. Modest reform should not be a substitute for challenging reform but rather a tactical move on the way to challenging reform. The key for most schools, once achieving Stage Two, is avoiding sliding back to Stage One while vigorously preparing to move to Stage Three. Modest reform will be inadequate for these tasks for most schools.

The journalist David Brooks, speaking of "the culture of debt" that contributed to the financial scandals and crises of 2008, alluded to a time of "reckoning."[1] Although the dimensions of the student cheating problem may not be as catastrophic, a time of reckoning is due in education that is going to require modest reform at a minimum. We have much knowledge of the student cheating problem, and this book has covered the gamut of it. What is needed now is well-constructed strategic action that is initiated responsibly and executed with discipline and steadfastness. David Brooks ended his article on debts with the following – "as the saying goes: people don't change when they see the light. They change when they feel the heat." So also with confronting student cheating.

We have argued throughout this book that the main leverage in confronting student cheating comes in the direct relationship between teaching and student learning. The rhetorical framework of linking more tightly the teaching and learning missions in education as a "pivot" is a key to student academic integrity and reminds teachers and faculty of their own professional commitments as scholars, mentors, coaches, evaluators, and assessors. For teachers and faculty, student academic integrity becomes an extension of their professionalism. For students, their academic integrity is a sign of respect for their teachers and confidence that their peers will not try to gain unfair advantage by cheating. Research tells us that students who respect their teachers cheat less frequently. And teachers who articulate their expectations on academic integrity tend to have less cheating in their classes. All this helps to define success in the confrontation of student academic dishonesty.

We have already explored the short-term deterrents to cheating in Chapter 5 and outlined the long-term deterrents in Chapter 6. If the vision becomes centered on a rejuvenation of teaching and learning, what refinements of tactics and strategies should be considered? We suggest five robust strategies for implementing the vision and six tactics to increase the chances for success. We have alluded to all of these throughout this volume but now concentrate on an agenda that can powerfully advance the academic integrity movement. The remainder of the chapter specifies how key constituencies can implement the vision around the pivot of rejuvenating teaching and learning.

The Five Strategies for Implementing a Vision of Success

1. Articulate the vision by building the presidential platform, thinking nationally, and acting locally.
2. Publicly acknowledge cheating as corruption and embrace the vulnerability that comes with that public acknowledgment.
3. Highlight expectations of all parties and mutual interests in highlighting academic integrity and fighting the corruption that erupts from cheating.
4. Work toward the institutionalization of academic integrity by making an academic integrity initiative a key strategic goal in our schools.
5. Embed academic integrity in the assessment and accreditation processes to create a formal mechanism for external accountability.

The Six Key Tactics for Pursuing the Strategies

1. Put public pressure on campus leaders (presidents and principals) and governing bodies (school boards, school districts, boards of trustees and boards of governors).
2. Avoid the allure of student-run honor codes and choose the policy and symbols that best match the campus culture.

3. Ensure defense mechanisms are in place for when progress slows or reverses.
4. Secure foundation support of experiments and initiatives on teaching excellence, academic integrity, and the integration of the multiple educational missions;
5. Summon the value of courage as a sixth value of academic integrity.
6. Internationalize the academic integrity movement.

While we have spoken to the first four tactics throughout the book, some elaboration on both courage and internationalization is needed. First to courage.

The moral vocabulary surrounding the academic integrity movement did not privilege "courage" as a value. For the Center for Academic Integrity's Fundamental Values Project, a key assumption related to courage prefaced the five values (responsibility, respect, fairness, honesty, and trustworthiness), but was not listed with them. Whatever the reason or reasons for not including courage on the list a decade ago, the post-9/11 world and the challenges of global climate change, financial crises, and economic dislocation certainly have emphasized the need for political will and, in President Obama's words, "the audacity of hope." Those who pay attention to the problem of student academic dishonesty already know, of course, about how it takes courage to confront a friend who cheats or a principal or dean who does not take cheating seriously (or even worse – does not support those who do). The courage we are talking about in our list above is more similar to political will than the everyday challenges of confronting student academic dishonesty. It is about politicizing the issue, mobilizing sustained public pressure on it, and demanding accountability from the educational establishment. College presidents, governing boards, and accreditation agencies are the "axis of possibility," and it is they – in particular – who must show courage. Shame and embarrassment alone cannot trigger it; it must come from both public pressure and the accumulation of knowledge and research on the problem. The last 15-year period has supplied the latter; we may only have the next 15 years for the former before a crisis of institutional confidence, like that affecting financial institutions in 2008, becomes a tsunami in education. Educators and political leaders will be unable to say they were not warned.

Now, more on the internationalization of the academic integrity movement. Though differences exist among countries regarding the understanding of, and propensity for, cheating (as we saw in an earlier chapter), the globalization of education requires that the movement to reduce cheating and enhance academic integrity be international. Students do not only attend schools in their own countries; and the United States, Australia, Britain, and Canada in particular admit a significant number of students from schools and colleges in other parts of the world. The international component of education, and higher education in particular, demands that, at the very least, institutions develop the capacity to respond to different cultural attitudes toward cheating. There is a growing awareness of the problem of student cheating around the world, and the Center for Academic Integrity has slowly seen an expansion of its membership outside of the United States. In addition, the popular and influential International Baccalaureate organization has attempted to draw its membership's attention toward the student cheating problem.[2]

Given that the US model of education is rapidly spreading worldwide, particularly in postsecondary education, it is likely that the growing US attention to student cheating will spread with it. This is going to be a complicated process with many unforeseen consequences. Internationalization of the academic integrity movement is virtually inevitable but its forms and variety of impacts are only now being anticipated. Of the six tactics listed, internationalization of the academic integrity movement is the one whose direction is most uncertain yet may need to be upgraded to a strategy. Much research needs to be conducted on cross-cultural attributes before internationalization can migrate to the status of a strategy, however. Small beginnings can be seen in various parts of the world, but what is needed internationally is the same kind of flowering of research on academic integrity that began in the United States in the 1990s and continues to this day. (More on the power and promise of research at the end of this chapter.)

We now turn to the key constituencies and how they can act in concert to stem the tide of student cheating and apply the strategies and tactics.

What Can Parents Do?

1. Use the experiences of homework as an opportunity to talk about the proper and improper relationships associated with collaboration with fellow students.

2. Quiz teachers on Parent–Teacher Association nights about how academic integrity/honesty is protected and advanced at schools.

3. Seize the teachable moment when your child has been found to have engaged in academic misconduct and help her accept responsibility and the consequences of her actions, rather than attempt to make the problem go away.

4. De-emphasize the importance of high grades for your child and emphasize the importance of learning, growing and discovering his intellectual and educational interests.

5. Encourage your child to seek out help from her teachers or teaching assistants if she's having trouble; teach her that there are honest alternatives to solving problems.

6. Help your child develop time management skills and avoid overscheduling, which can often lead to cheating. Establish set times for completing homework and prioritize school work over other activities.

7. At the elementary and secondary levels of education, keep open communication lines with your child's teachers and school administrators; understand how assignments are expected to be completed and express questions or concerns about the curricula.

8. At the college or university level, encourage your student to understand the school's academic integrity policy or honor

code and help to ensure that he understands the value of the lower grade honestly earned over the higher grade earned through cheating.

9. Be cognizant of pressures on your student to get "good grades" – scholarships, financial aid, dreams of college or postgraduate education. These pressures can lead to cheating, but an awareness of this can help your child resist the temptation to put goals ahead of integrity.

What Can Teachers Do?

In secondary education:

1. Talk to students several times a semester on the importance of academic integrity and candidly about the temptations to cheat.
2. In partnership with parents, "engage our children in a conversation about information ethics and teach them about the principles of copyright law. It's important, however, that we teach our kids not only what they are not allowed to do, but also to show them what can be done with content in ethically sound and lawful ways."[3]
3. Make sure academic integrity is on the agenda annually at teacher orientation and development sessions.
4. Verify that principals and assistant principals have a protocol for dealing with cheating allegations that is user friendly for teachers and fair to students.
5. Make sure that there is a written policy and procedure that is shared with students and parents, to ensure that everyone is "on the same page".
6. Teach students *why* we cite and acknowledge sources, and show them how to properly do it. Reward them for proper citation practices.

7. Delineate the difference between authorized use of resources and deceptive use to get assignments done. Teach them that "by any means" is not the integrous way.

8. Encourage tempered parental involvement – parents should not be doing their children's work, and clamp down on parents when they do.

In colleges and universities:

1. Reduce opportunities for cheating by attending to crowded examination conditions and ensuring that assessments and assignments are meaningful and fair.

2. Be clear on syllabi that academic integrity is important to you and what is or is not permitted in terms of collaboration on team exercises, projects, or homework.

3. Talk to students several times a semester about academic integrity.

4. Share with your students the intellectual origins and sources of lecture materials; in other words, model how you stand on the shoulders of the intellectuals who came before you.

5. Consistently report students who do violate your campus integrity policy so they can learn what constitutes acceptable and unacceptable behavior.

6. Push academic senate (faculty government) and campus administration to make academic integrity a strategic priority.

What Can Academic Administrators Do?

1. Include academic integrity policies and procedures in all orientation programs, for students, faculty, adjunct faculty, and staff.

2. Make sure that your academic integrity policies and procedures are clear and user friendly for faculty.

3. Create a network of liaisons in departments who are champions of integrity and a resource for their close colleagues.

4. Be conscious about what stage of institutionalization your school is at and communicate that consistently to faculty.

5. Support faculty improvement of teaching by awarding course release time for course development, and points toward tenure and promotion for improved teaching.

6. Ensure adequate teaching support staff to help grade assignments and proctor examinations.

7. Support faculty who report academic misconduct by ignoring low, outlying course evaluations in semesters when a faculty has reported student cheating.

8. Reach out to allies among students and student affairs professionals who can help educate students about academic integrity.

9. Offer incentives for the development of ethics programs, courses, and initiatives.

10. Help reduce opportunities for cheating by scheduling exams in sufficiently sized rooms so that faculty can space out students, or schedule finals in large halls where students testing in different subject areas can be altered in the seats.

What Can Principals and Presidents Do?

1. Demand that there be good data on cheating rates on campus, a common understanding of what stage of institutionalization the school is at, and a plan to protect progress and/or move to a higher level of institutionalization.

2. Make academic integrity a consistent part of the "story" of your campus, its role in teaching and research missions, and its value to students, faculty, alumni, and society in general.
3. Insist that assessment and self-studies on campus include attention to academic integrity.
4. Signal a clarity of expectations yet modesty of purpose that is both realistic and demanding.
5. Meet with some students and faculty who have been immersed in cheating allegations after the experience to listen to what they say about it.
6. Explore with foundations how the issue of academic integrity can be insinuated into their themes.

College or university presidents must step up their leadership profiles in regard to academic integrity. There is a need for the matter of student academic honesty to be discussed beyond presidents and boards of trustees at honor-code schools. Presidents, of course, have a multitude of expectations on them that draw them in a variety of directions. It is critical, however, that the layer of academic leaders below president, that is academic vice-presidents and deans, has optimism about how their institutions can respond to student academic dishonesty, and their optimism includes faculty action to address the problem.

The role of presidents is essential in guiding institutions to take the issue of student academic dishonesty more seriously. Tim Dodd, former director of the Center for Academic Integrity, stated in 2007: "It has to happen at the presidential level. We don't see presidents gathering at the conference and their symposia, saying, 'We need to take a hard look at this.' The way they embraced multiculturalism years ago, the way they embraced internationalism, they need to come together and embrace integrity."[4]

A big part of the challenge for academic leaders, including presidents, seems to be in understanding how coordinated action occurs on campus and how a process of institutionalizing academic integrity can take place. Benchmarks seem to be needed and commonly understood. Also needed are ways to comprehend the inevitable reversals of progress which will happen as progress on institutionalization occurs.

What Can Governing and School Board Members Do?

1. Ask presidents/superintendents about what level of institutionalization the campus is at and what is being done about it.
2. Bring up the topic of academic integrity with donors, alumni, and friends of the school to gauge reactions and to communicate concern on the topic.
3. Provide support to presidents/principals to ensure institutional integrity, for example: ensure consistency between rhetoric and practice; reduce class sizes; match the attention paid to teaching and learning with its espoused importance; and, monitor administrative, research, and teaching misconduct to the same level as student cheating.
4. Back up teachers and schools that clamp down on student cheating and resist parental pressure to overlook cheating incidents.

What Can Advocacy Groups Do?

1. The Center for Academic Integrity and Josephson Institute for Ethics, for example, should develop stronger linkages so as to coordinate their actions in advancing academic integrity.
2. As suggested by David Callahan,[5] bring the issue of academic integrity more directly to the political process by

    lobbying key legislators who have their own interests – personally, professionally and politically – on issues of character, moral leadership, and the future of education.

3. Extend organizational efforts internationally more aggressively, as the CAI has already done in Canada.

4. Be the public voice against cheating and for academic integrity by publishing white papers, writing op-eds, and speaking out in other popular press venues.

5. Garner corporate support for academic integrity by encouraging employers to value integrity over grades and donate monies to help the cause.

One could even argue, as has Daniel Callahan, that advocacy for academic integrity could stall if solid organizational action and commitments do not come forward in the very near future.

What Can External Agencies Do?

1. Accrediting agencies can demand statistics on cheating and corruption.

2. Assessment agencies can require that schools measure student cheating, specifically in connection with student learning, institutional structures, teacher behaviors, and institutional culture.

3. Transparency International, or other agencies like it that measure integrity or corruption, could consider student cheating as corruption and rate educational institutions around the world on their integrity value.

4. Popular university rating systems such as those published by the *U.S. News & World Report*, *Macleans* magazine (Canada), and the World University Ranking should include academic integrity as an important factor.

5. Foundations can provide funding to assist advocacy groups, such as the Center for Academic Integrity, and

support academic integrity research. The William and Flora Hewlett Foundation was crucial to the CAI in the development of the Fundamental Values Project that crafted a key moral vocabulary for academic integrity. And the Templeton Foundation did something similar when it funded the assessment project for CAI which has begun to be used in higher education.

Regional accreditation agencies develop rules and processes for colleges and universities to engage in thorough self-studies and external reviews, typically every five to ten years. The self-studies cover everything from finances to facilities to governance processes along with the effectiveness and suitability of curriculum including that of general education. These self-studies are massive, and large amounts of data are collected and analyzed. But it is curious that data on student cheating rates and how a campus is dealing with it are not expected to be included or voluntarily collected. Accreditation standards do speak to the issue of integrity but the statements are very general and rarely does one see attention to the student academic dishonesty problem in the self-studies. Pressure by state governments led to assessment being included in regional accreditation standards. But assessment of student academic dishonesty will not likely occur without significant and prolonged public pressure to do so.

Another source of pressure on accreditation agencies could come from voluntary activities of colleges and universities to assess their academic integrity systems and then include the data and analysis in their self-studies. There has been some movement in this direction as the Center for Academic Integrity, funded by the Templeton Foundation, helped organize methodical assessment practices which have been used by a number of campuses. Institutions can be persuaded to include these in their accreditation self-studies and, if some of the schools have been chosen as model self-studies, it is possible that accreditation will begin to take the student cheating issue seriously. Public pressure is still required, of course, but this may be an important start.

Summary

While these key constituencies can and should act to contain student cheating and advance the cause of academic integrity, there was one we did not list specifically: schools of education. We did not include them because of their lack of potential influence. But schools of education are like the "dog that does not bark" in the Sherlock Holmes story. Holmes solved a case by noting that a dog that did not bark gave the important clue to solving a mystery. Likewise, we have written an entire volume on student cheating to this point without alluding to a group that has reach from K-12 all the way through graduate education. Several individual researchers have emerged from schools of education to study academic integrity, but an organized, high-level scholarly effort has not matured there nor been stimulated by foundation grants. There are many possible explanations including the exigencies of producing sufficient teachers and school administrators to handle the all-too-daunting need for trained personnel along with the greater traction of the character education movement in schools of education. But why not sustained attention to academic integrity itself given the centrality of the cheating issue in the direct pedagogical process?

There are at least two more ways to answer that question. The first is promising: schools of education await the accumulated pressure and concerns of the constituencies above before they take on the task in earnest. The second is less promising: schools of education are so inundated by other pressures and bureaucratic inertia that they cannot become central players in the academic integrity movement. It is the view and hope of the authors that the first answer is stronger, and that schools of education and foundations will respond to the concerted efforts of other key constituencies in the decade to come.

The Power and Promise of Research

Although there has been a surge of research in the last 15 years on student cheating, more needs to be done and it should be widespread. More dissertations are being done on academic integrity than a generation ago. And there are new subdisciplines such as behavioral economics which hold great promise in finding ways to structure better choices for students. An important recent book by two scholars at the University Chicago, Richard Thaler and Cass Sunstein, apply what they call "libertarian paternalism" to an array of choices about "health, wealth, and happiness" (part of the sub-title of their book, *Nudge*).[6] They seek what they call "good choice architecture" to help people make better decisions. While behavioral economics has not been applied yet to the problem of student cheating, it will no doubt happen. The beauty of this approach is that it will likely bridge the gap between challenging reform and modest reform which we discussed earlier. Conceptualizing ways to induce better student choices without massive organizational efforts holds great power and promise.

But research needs to be more widespread to throw both heat and light on the student cheating problem. There are three major weaknesses in the current body of research on academic integrity that must be addressed if we hope to generate new knowledge and understandings. First, while there has been much research conducted, it is largely disconnected by disciplinary boundaries, countries of origin, and publishing outlets. Thus, it can take a significant amount of effort to find all of the research that has been published; even though the three authors have written several articles, book chapters, and a dissertation before engaging in this book project, they still uncovered research on cheating and academic integrity that they had not seen before! A central database of academic integrity research, popular press articles, and white papers must be created; such a database can stimulate future research and creative thinking on still-needed data.

Second, the majority of research conducted has focused on the internal and organizational dimensions of the student cheating problem. Research on the internal dimension examines academic integrity/ academic dishonesty at the level of the individual student, conceiving the problem as one of deviant behavior and the solution as primarily about character and cognitive development. Research on the organizational dimension examines academic conduct as largely shaped by facets of the organization, such as classroom dynamics and peer culture, and views the solution to academic misconduct to be the creation of integrity cultures. Research on the institutional dimension (the factors of the larger educational system that shape the academic conduct of students) and societal dimension (which would critique the changing views of knowledge, authorship, misconduct, and integrity, and how these views shape student behaviors) is far less common. We need research conducted on all four dimensions to really understand the problem and possible solutions.

And, finally, research on academic integrity and student cheating has not been widely supported by associations, agencies, and funding sources. There are trends in educational research, and those most common have been on other critical issues such as higher education access, community colleges, diversity and equity, and financial aid. A cursory review of annual conference programs from the period of 1992 (when the Center for Academic Integrity was established) to 2008 for such influential associations as the American Education Research Association (AERA), Association for the Study of Higher Education (ASHE), NASPA (Student Affairs Administrators in Higher Education) reveals a paucity of presentations and sessions on the topic. It may be slightly of a "chicken and egg" problem; until more agencies are funding research on academic integrity, academics may not conduct research, but until academics are conducting the research, funding agencies are unlikely to fund.

What can be done to increase the amount and expand the breadth of research conducted on academic integrity and academic cheating? Public pressure on schools of education professors to answer questions about the problem and propose solutions may incite more faculty to conduct research (if not purely from embarrassment at their lack of knowledge on the topic). Colleges and universities could support internal research and perhaps even offer modest grants (such as course-release time) to encourage faculty to conduct academic integrity research projects. State and federal governments, if strongly advocated, may be convinced to provide monetary support for research, and advocacy groups, like the Center for Academic Integrity, could convince more grant agencies to fund research if they can manage to politicize the issue and popularize it in public discourse. Associations, agencies, and governments like to be on the cutting edge of hot topics and to be at the front of nationally recognized movements; we just need to convince them that academic integrity could be that hot topic and that movement is possible.

Conclusion

Research on student academic dishonesty can be a marvelous stimulus to conversation and action, and we encourage it at all levels. Research is at the heart of the fifth strategy we identified in the beginning of the chapter. But research can be more expansive than just assessment and re-accreditation self-studies. Even undergraduates can conduct research on academic integrity as Steve Davis has shown. Not only does student research open up conversations, but it teaches students about proper research techniques and attribution of sources. How's that for killing two birds with one stone!

Chapter 9

An Optimistic (and Provocative) Conclusion

Finding the Good in Student Cheating

Some have argued that the United States is losing its competitive position in the world because of moral decay and weak schools. This popular opinion is not supported by facts, however. Journalist Fareed Zakaria notes that, particularly for higher education, the United States has distinct advantages in both quality and access over the rest of the world.[1] Zakaria argues that our K-12 system is itself "in the middle of the pack,"[2] and he gives evidence from the highly regarded Trends in International Mathematics and Science Study. But Zakaria's main point is that American education succeeds mostly because "it is very good at developing critical faculties of the mind."[3] He quotes Singapore's education minister who admires the United States emphasis on "creativity, curiosity" and even the "culture of learning that challenges conventional wisdom" including "challenging authority."[4]

What if we could see student acceptance of cheating as a symbol of the strengths of education – creativity and the challenging of conventions and authority? This is not to rationalize cheating, of course, but rather to see another facet of this multifaceted phenomenon. Finding a good in bad behavior does not justify the behavior but helps us understand the culture and motivations of students. Imagine the following conversation between two students, which illustrates the rebelliousness theme:

STUDENT A: This next calculus exam is stupid – the prof himself said we'll never have to use this technique again.

STUDENT B: I know – that is why even Jenny is thinking of sneaking a crib sheet in.

STUDENT A: Can't really blame her. We needed to have spent far more time on the earlier material.

STUDENT B: It's tempting, I guess. Hope she doesn't get caught – she's the smartest kid in the class.

This is a teachable moment, among students, and could be anticipated by a dedicated professor who understands the pressures on students as well as their resourcefulness and creativity in meeting what they see as the goals of the education "game" – getting the assignments done. Such a faculty would see the need for discussing the value of his specific lesson plans so that students will consider not just the goal of assignment completion, but the value of the learning process. In this example, it seems, authority needed to be challenged, and the students would have benefited with more options to do so in legitimate ways. A great education does not lead to the stamping out of curiosity nor to complete deference to professors and teachers. The goal of education, after all, is not to graduate uncritical and complacent "drones," but dynamic and critical thinkers who can solve some of the most complex problems facing society.

So, let's push ourselves to consider the good in Jenny's decision to cheat, that is, her willingness to challenge authority. The bad in her decision is her lack of courage (there's that word again) to challenge authority in a direct, honest, and transparent manner. (Of course, to find the good in student cheating, we must acknowledge that students, on their own, often lack the power to challenge authority in more ethical ways.) Thus, if Jenny had cheated, what would be most important is her understanding that she made an unethical choice when she actually had several more ethical choices at her disposal (e.g., overtly challenging the teacher or speaking with the department chair). This is evidence of both the good and the bad of student cheating. Finding the good does not help us rationalize the bad but rather helps us understand it in a way that has layers of meaning beyond that of enforcement of a prohibition.

The Search for Meaning

To search for greater meaning in this example, we turn for a moment to a classic tale on rebelliousness and the limitations of authoritarian responses to it. This classic tale centers on the time of the Spanish Inquisition and imagines what would happen if Christ returned and was arrested by the grand inquisitor. In this story, by the famous Russian novelist Fyodor Dostoevsky, the inquisitor lectures Christ on how he – Christ – had not read human nature well and why humans needed authority to provide for their happiness and an elite to discipline their rebellious tendencies.[5] Although Christ does not respond verbally in the scene, the reader understands the level of satire and is implicitly invited to argue with the inquisitor on Christ's behalf. We know, after all, that human beings respond more positively to the "audacity of hope" than they do to the threat of fear and punishment. To be sure, and we have argued this already, there does need to be costs associated with morally reprehensible behaviors, both so people know that the behavior is reprehensible and so we can maintain some semblance of social order. But fear more often paralyzes while hope motivates, and we hope that the readers are more interested in inspiring active academic integrity, thinking and learning, than they are obsessively repressing cheating (and thus, risking also the loss of creativity, challenge, critical thinking, and learning).

Finding the good in rebelliousness is not only a theme of literature (and many Hollywood movies) but a feature of much modern social and political thought. Likewise, if student cheating is always seen as a problem and a glass half empty, it will be hard to imagine it more positively and as a glass mostly full. There are deep psychological and philosophical attributes to the student cheating problem that we have only touched on since our effort has been to seek practical paths from the most current research and scholarship on student cheating. But our conclusion does pick up on irony, that is, confronting and sublimating student cheating by understanding it and, in many ways, accepting it as reality. This is more than using "teaching moments" when confronting cheaters or those who enable them (including teachers, parents, administrators, and educational leaders); rather, it is a broader embrace and comprehension of the student cheating phenomenon so as to supply a perspective on student cheating which brings together, in a very human way, the power and promise of confronting student academic dishonesty. This, like stimulating research on student cheating, opens up larger conversations about student cheating and informs the power and promise of confronting student cheating.

Now back to Jenny. Imagine if the teachable moment of Jenny and her friends evolved in the following way:

STUDENT A: You are right; she is the smartest in the class. Maybe she should think again – preparing a crib sheet is more work for her than just learning that technique. Let's tell her that and sketch out something else.

STUDENT B: What do you have in mind?

STUDENT A: The professor seems like a decent guy. Why don't we just tell them that we are not as motivated as well for this test because of what he said about never using this calculus technique again? We could ask him if he would reconsider the weight of this exam. After all, he did postpone the first quiz by two days when he knew we weren't ready.

STUDENT B: I guess it is worth a shot. He might learn something about how to package this part of the course even if he gets irritated with us. Let's talk with Jenny.

STUDENT A: Jenny, you have been bothered by this upcoming exam as much as us. We have an idea. Why don't we just tell the prof we are struggling with this material because we know we won't be using it again?

JENNY: You'd be willing to do that? What if he gets mad at us?

Finding the Good in Student Cheating

STUDENT A: I bet he won't – he's been helpful in office hours although his lectures are somewhat boring.

STUDENT B: He might be willing to come up with some ideas about how to deal with our frustration. Sometimes it's better than just asking a prof to do something he'd rather not do. He could think up some options or at least explain better why this technique could be useful.

JENNY: I guess it's worth a go – what are his office hours today?

The professor has several options in responding to the students when they come in. One is the authoritarian posture of the inquisitor: "I know this material best, and this is the way it is done." But good professors have more empathy than that and know how to tap student potential and indeed their rebelliousness. He need not have suspected that his students were considering cheating. And, even if he did, it need not have reinforced an authoritarian tendency in the professor. This session with the students gives the professor information that can improve his responsiveness and effectiveness as a teacher *and* at relatively little cost to him.

Imagine, in comparison, a similar situation in a country known for its rigid, hierarchic classrooms where students are motivated to succeed, where deference to teachers is strictly expected, and where critical thinking skills are not an educational priority.

STUDENT A: This next calculus exam is stupid – the professor told us to memorize this new technique but tells us we will never use it again.

STUDENT B: Big deal – all you have to do is memorize it and get through the exam.

STUDENT A: That will take hours, and I have a big economics exam the same day.

STUDENT B: So why are you wasting time chatting with me?

STUDENT A: Because you had the same problem in a course last year, and you got away with that crib sheet. I want to try that – show me how you did it.

STUDENT B: I guess it is not hard to do. Let me show you – you're right, the exam is stupid. Why not?

211

The rebelliousness of these students is easy to understand, and they see their situation starkly: work very hard on memorization or cheat. There is little in the educational structure to provide student input to the professor, and there are few outlets for rebelliousness. The choice for teachers is often misconstrued everywhere as being "easy" or "tough" on students. The choice should be seen as creative and skillful, that is, how do I as a teacher combine high standards with greater knowledge of the pace and pattern of student learning? One of the perceived dangers of "no child left behind" in the United States is that measurable standards will dilute the nurturing of critical skills by inducing teachers to exaggerated attention to scores and testing. Higher education in the United States has had less of this than K-12, and it will be fascinating to see the consequences of no child left behind in the "pipelines" to enrollment in colleges and universities. Whether the rest of the world will become "more like us"[6] or we like them in education will be watched closely, and academic integrity will be part of the equation both in the United States and in the rest of the world.

Throughout this volume we have suggested that the power and promise of confronting student cheating are in the affirmation and rejuvenation of teaching. Experienced teachers and professors intuitively yet methodically realize that proactive approaches are more efficient than reactive ones. Good teaching assumes the possibilities of student cheating; but, more importantly, it anticipates something else – the energy, creativity, and, yes, the rebelliousness of students. Teachers convert this to learning by finding the good in students including even the possibilities that their students will be tempted to cheat.

The Search for Meaning II

"There are a terrible lot of lies going about the world, and the worst of it is that half of them are true."

Winston Churchill

Jeremy Campbell in *The Liar's Tale* explores the many ways lying manifests itself. He begins by using examples from the work of Charles Darwin. Nature, in Campbell's words, may be "harboring a propensity for cheating".[7] In a competitive world it can be argued that "fraud is a positive asset".[8] We are all familiar with the old saying that "all's fair in love and war." Even after saying it, a person normally recognizes the hyperbole in this. Yet we know that lying – and its close cousin, cheating – occurs frequently. But lying rarely occurs all the time in an individual's behavior, except perhaps with a pathological liar, and the statistics on student cheating show that 75 percent of students cheat infrequently (with the exception of homework). Earlier in the volume we identified the curse of short-term thinking in which calculations of the game by cutting corners in the near term overwhelmed the clear advantages of not cutting corners for the long term in acquiring professional skills. So where can you find much good in all of this?

Campbell argues that "lying is a necessity of life" and "is part of the terrifying and problematic character of existence. We have come full circle from the ancient thesis that truth and goodness are inseparable twins".[9] At least since Machiavelli – as we shall see shortly – our cultures and politics have dealt with this assertion that truth and goodness are not necessarily coterminous, but we often do not deal with it well. Activists in higher education, in particular, either bemoan the division between the pursuits of the good and true or celebrate the liberation of the human spirit by accepting the division.[10]

The academic integrity movement has tended to avoid the topic by soft assumptions that pursuit of truth and pursuit of the good could easily be reconciled. Rather than seeing easy reconciliation, it is better to accept the reality that even the highest ideals of the academy, by themselves, cannot develop goodness for our students. "Goodness" has to be managed, nurtured, and integrated into our educational systems, at least in terms of reliably validating student performance. It is a limited goal, to be sure, but that in turn makes it easier to get there from here.

Machiavelli and the Realists

There is arguably no one more renowned for defending the skills of dissembling and deception than the sixteenth century Florentine diplomat, Niccolò Machiavelli. He found a good in the politics of lying, but even he knew that, if it occurred constantly, it lost its effectiveness. Campbell said something similar when he stated "that in a system which draws much of its strength from candor, lies are all the more effective, all the more insidious".[11] Student cheating has the same quality; it is insidious because it is not done all the time by all students and is particularly inimical to the transmission of knowledge and validation of student achievement. The purpose of this book is to flag the problem of student cheating and to suggest comprehensive ways of dealing with it. Would it not be a delicious irony to end a book about confronting student cheating by using Machiavelli to help us not only find the good in student cheating but also create and invent ways to maximize that good?

Machiavelli's *Discourses* are a treasure trove of reflections on how to be effective in politics and government. For Machiavelli, goodness is a condition of most people in uncorrupted societies or a consequence of effective government. Political leaders should be effective rather than good. For Machiavelli, people "very rarely know how to be completely bad or completely good".[12] By accepting this, one can begin to define oneself as a realist. Machiavelli, like Dostoevsky, knew that rebelliousness, if bottled up, created "disorder".[13] And it was order that Machiavelli saw as the greatest good. This required, then, both effectiveness and responsiveness. Finding the right balance is an art and a skill; likewise for teachers.

Machiavelli is also known for his instruction that the end justifies the means. It is really a call for thinking strategically first and then tactically. But, as self-proclaimed political realist Saul Alinsky said in the 1970s, it is primarily about pursuing a "*particular* end" with "*particular* means."[14] Alinsky spoke of his own optimism; and, while Machiavelli is known for his pessimistic view of human nature, it is his understanding that political skill and inventiveness could produce a successful republic. Finding the right balance of optimism and pessimism is important in politics, and it is essential for teachers.

But what is the end for teachers? The learning assessment movement has been pronounced in all levels of education. It is often seen by educators as a political imposition. In fact it is a thorny reminder that educators have not been especially adept about defining the *particular* ends of their pedagogies and how those ends are to be measured. Student cheating and educator manipulation of test results can confound this process. The overarching end for teachers is a vision and goal of an *order* that can accommodate whatever sets of learning goals that are established. It requires responsiveness to the characteristics – both positive and negative – of students and effectiveness in meeting those goals and the expectations of parents and the broader society. It is beyond the scope of this volume to sketch all of the facets of this order. Three facets of educational *disorder* have been identified, however: *a high incidence of student cheating*; *inattention* or sporadic attention *to student cheating*; and, *uncoordinated responses to student cheating*. Diminishing disorder produces order, according to Machiavelli, if citizens can "vent their feeling".[15] Likewise in education. Understanding and making possible legitimate ways to "vent" the rebelliousness that leads to student cheating are essential if education is to be effective while avoiding the disorder attached to corruption. Like Machiavelli and Alinsky, we have approached the topic in this volume as practically and realistically as possible. Throughout, we have established areas meant to accomplish the desired end of an uncorrupted order in our educational systems. A not insignificant means has been asserting the importance and utility of conversations in understanding and confronting the problem of student cheating. Instigating "discourses" was also Machiavelli's technique, too, of course.

Saul Alinsky also talked of the power and promise for both conversations and the Socratic method as means to an end for community organizers. In a chapter entitled "In the Beginning" in his 1971 volume, *Rules for Radicals*,[16] Alinsky gives an extended example of how an organizer could use this method to help a slum dweller confront a slum owner. We conclude our volume with a similar conversation that can be an example to all those who should care deeply about education and the cultivation of integrity. While the old saying, "values are caught not taught" may apply, it is essential that we establish places and moments as "catchments." What follows is a conversation beginning with a question from a faculty champion of student academic integrity to an academic dean.

FACULTY CHAMPION (FC):	How do you handle the fact that most of your faculty are ignoring our college policy by not turning in cases of student cheating? They are deciding to handle it completely on their own and in an isolated way while ignoring the clear, published policy that requires them to turn it into you – and the faculty themselves established the policy 10 years ago!
DEAN:	We have a few cases turned in each year, but the grapevine tells me also that the policy is being ignored, as you say.
FC:	You are wallowing in this and being hypocritical. Why not eliminate our academic integrity policy and procedures altogether and let faculty individually do what they want?! They are doing it anyway! Your cynicism is outrageous!
DEAN:	You know faculty. They see their control of the classroom as academic freedom. It is sacred, and they are talented individuals. It is very, very difficult to get them to see the consequences of not flagging those students so that other faculty can be protected. They really don't care.
FC:	Yet our faculty take pride in being good teachers!
DEAN:	And they are! But what is in it for them to follow the policy?
FC:	Maybe you have to confront them – I am sure that slumlords think they are doing a favor for the residents. Should we let slumlords off the hook?
DEAN:	Don't be absurd! Faculty are not like slumlords.

FC: Okay – let me show you. Slumlords provide a service – relatively inexpensive housing – and turn it into a decent living for themselves. Are you the slum dweller or the slumlord? You supply decent education – you could be the slumlord – or you could be the slum dweller, just living in appalling conditions *because you think you can't do anything about it.*

DEAN: Come on. This college is not a slum.

FC: If you have these high cheating rates, why not consider it slimy, even disgusting. Just because we have a beautiful quadrangle does not mean we are not like a slum!

DEAN: You're pushing this too far.

FC: Am I? You are just pretending to be a slum dweller, I think, to avoid responsibility. You really are more like a slumlord, I think! That is your secret!

DEAN: Enough of this. Your moralism is unrealistic.

FC: Let me ask you. You think you can clean this up? It may take less effort than you think. What would you do first or don't you care?

DEAN: Of course I care! What do you think I should do first?

FC: Read this book!

A Final Note

Despite the emotions in the conversation above, it is possible to imagine a myriad of productive conversations across the spectrum from advocates of student academic honesty to cynics like the dean above. This book has attempted to supply the components of those conversations. We have tried to affirm the thinking of the advocates while understanding the hesitations of the cynics.

Finding the right balance of optimism and pessimism is one of the keys to advancing the quest for greater student academic honesty. Advocates of academic integrity often speak of the "crisis" or "epidemic" of student cheating. But beneath this rhetoric there is a deep optimism that students, faculty, administrators, parents, and citizens can make a difference. To listen to students at an honor-code school or students who attend the annual meeting of the Center for Academic Integrity is to be immersed in an optimism that borders on heroic and is contagious despite the well-understood scale and depth of the problem of student academic dishonesty. Besides finding the right balance of optimism and pessimism – and it should lean in the direction of the optimism – the message of this book is that the pursuit of student academic honesty in the end comes down to four main themes or *musts*:

1. It must be *coordinated* among educational stakeholders.
2. It must be *persistent*.
3. It must be supported by *scholarship and research*.
4. It must be informed by prudential and sophisticated judgments about using academic integrity as a *key pivot* in a renaissance of teaching and learning in our schools.

The historic moment is right – do we dare not try?

Notes

Chapter 1   Cheating in Our Schools, Colleges, and Universities

1   A high school student speaking with journalist Regan McMahon in McMahon, Regan (2007, September 9). "Everybody does it: Academic cheating is at an all-time high. Can anything be done to stop it?" *San Francisco Gate*. Retrieved from www.sfgate.com, September 9, 2007.

2   Owen, Glen, 2003 (October 7), "It's true, parents do pupils' homework," *The Times* of London. Retrieved July 15, 2007 from *ProQuest Historical Newspapers*.

3   Wolk, Ronald A., 2000 (February 1), "Quiz show," *Teacher Magazine*. Retrieved April 30, 2008 from www.teachermagazine.org.

4   http://dictionary.reference.com/browse/cheating

5   See one version of the story at http://www.plagiarismtoday.com/2008/08/26/the-biden-plagiarism-scandal/

6   We acknowledge that not all students engage in these behaviors with the *intent* to deceive. In particular, plagiarism has been eloquently described as a problem that may more often stem from ignorance or writing difficulties. We do not address this distinction here as other writers have already done a fine job of that. See, for example, the writings by Rebecca Moore Howard of Syracuse University, and also those by Lisa Maruca of Wayne State University.

7   Pope, Justin, 2007 (June 3), "Theme of dishonesty runs beneath recent college headlines," *North County Times*, G-3.

8   Owen, Glen, 2003.

9   We acknowledge that some may argue whether schools should do this and whether they actually do that now. We also acknowledge that student cheating is not the only thing that undermines or corrupts this role of schools – unfair and inaccurate assessments, poor teaching and assessment, and so on also do. By emphasizing student cheating we do not mean to minimize the impact of those, but to focus on one particular poignant issue. We encourage all readers to consider the problems together.

10 Heyneman, Stephen, P., 2004. "Education and corruption," *International Journal of Educational Development*, 24(6): 637–48.

11 Vojak, Colleen, 2006, "What market culture teaches students about ethical behavior," *Ethics and Education*, 1(2): 177–95.

12 Friedman, Benjamin M., 2005, *The Moral Consequences of Economic Growth*, New York: Knopf.

13 Hallak, Jacques, & Poisson, Muriel, 2007, *Corrupt Schools, Corrupt Universities: What Can be Done?* Paris: International Institute for Educational Planning.

14 See, for example: Slaughter, Sheila, & Leslie, Larry, L., 1999, *Academic Capitalism: Politics, Policies, and the Entrepreneurial University*, Baltimore, MD: Johns Hopkins University Press; Slaughter, Sheila & Rhodes, Gary, 2004, *Academic Capitalism and the New Economy: Markets, State, and Higher Education*, Baltimore, MD: Johns Hopkins University Press; Washburn, Jennifer, 2006, *University Inc: The Corporate Corruption of Higher Education*, New York: Basic Books.

15 Molnar, Alex & Garcia, David, R.,2005, *Empty Calories: Commercializing Activities in America's Schools*, Tempe, AZ: Education Policy Studies Laboratory. Available online at http://www.epicpolicy.org/files/EPSL-0511-103-CERU.pdf

16 Ibid.; Washburn, 2006.

17 Washburn, 2006, p. 240.

18 Ibid., p. 241.

19 Wellman, Jane, V., Desrochers, Donna, M., & Lenihan, Colleen, M., 2008, *The Growing Imbalance: Recent Trends in US Postsecondary Education Finance*, Washington, DC: The Delta Cost Project.

20 Ibid. and Guthrie, James, W., 1996, "Reinventing education finance: Alternatives for allocating resources to individual schools," Selected Papers

in School Finance. Retrieved May 1, 2008 from http://165.224.221.98/pubs98/guthrie.pdf.

21 Altbach, Philip, G., 1999, "The logic of mass higher education," *Tertiary Education and Management*, 5(2): 107–24.

22 Ibid.

23 Eckstein, Max A., 2003, *Combating Academic Fraud: Towards a Culture of Integrity*, Paris: International Institute for Educational Planning; Hallak & Poisson, 2007.

24 Bertram Gallant, Tricia, Beesemyer, Laurel A., & Kezar, Adrianna (in press). "Creating a culture of ethics in higher education," in J. C. Knapp and D. J. Siegel (eds.), *The Business of Higher Education*, Westport, CT: Praeger.

25 McClellan, B. Edward, 1999, *Moral Education in America: Schools and the Shaping of Character from Colonial Times to the Present*, New York: Teachers College Press, p. 71.

26 *An American Imperative: Higher Expectations for Higher Education*, Wingspread Group on Higher Education Report, The Johnson Foundation, 1993.

27 www.charactercounts.org/about/background.htm

28 www.charactercounts.org

29 *The Fundamental Values of Academic Integrity* booklet can be downloaded for free from www.academicintegrity.org

30 See Callahan, David, 2004, *The Cheating Culture: Why More Americans are Doing Wrong to Get Ahead*, New York: Harcourt Publishers.

31 McCabe, D. L., & Drinan, P., 1999 (October 15), "Toward a culture of academic integrity," *The Chronicle of Higher Education*.

32 Almond, Gabriel, A., & Verba, Sidney, 1989, *The Civic Culture: Political Attitudes and Democracy in Five Nations*, Thousand Oaks, CA: Sage Publications, p. 8.

Chapter 2 The Nature and Prevalence of Student Cheating

1 Josephson, Michael, 2008 (June 17), "Cheating isn't the problem." Retrieved November 25, 2008 from http://charactercounts.org/michael/2008/06/cheating_isnt_the_problem_5713.html

2 www.dictionary.com

3 McCabe, Donald L., 2005, "Cheating among college and university students: A North American perspective," *International Journal of Educational Integrity*, 1(1): 1–11 (p. 5).

4 McMahon, Regan, 2007 (September 9), "Everyone does it: Academic cheating is at an all-time high. Can anything be done to stop it?" *San Francisco Chronicle*. Retrieved from http://sfgate.com, February 5, 2008.

5 Sweeney, Nicole, 2004 (May 19), "Students armed with technology usher in a new school of cheating," *Milwaukee Journal Sentinel*. Retrieved from www.jsonline.com February 1, 2008.

6 "University fraud," 2007 (February 12), *Maclean's Magazine*. Retrieved June 12, 2007 from www.macleans.ca.

7 Satterlee, Anita G., 2002, "Academic dishonesty among students: Consequences and intervention." ERIC report, ED469468 (p. 3).

8 Pytel, B., 2007 (September 16), "Cheating is on the rise: Surveys show less integrity among high school and college students." Retrieved February 21, 2008 from http://classroom-issues.suite101.com/article.cfm/cheating_is_on_the_rise

9 Stothard, Michael, 2008 (October 31), "'1 in 2' admits to plagiarism," *Varsity*. Retrieved October 31, 2008 from www.varsity.co.uk.

10 McCabe, D. L., 2005.

11 Bertram Gallant, T., 2008, *Academic Integrity in the Twenty-First Century: A Teaching and Learning Imperative*, San Francisco: Jossey-Bass.

12 Angell, R. C., 1928, *The Campus: A Study of Contemporary Undergraduate Life in the American University*, New York: D. Appleton.

13 Drake, C. A., 1941, "Why students cheat," *The Journal of Postsecondary Education*, 12(8): 418–20; Parr, F. W. (1936), "The problem of student honesty," *The Journal of Postsecondary Education*, 7(6): 318–26.

14 Angell, 1928, p. 44.

15 Bertram Gallant, 2008.

16 McCabe, Donald L., & Bowers, William J., 1994, "Academic dishonesty among males in college: A thirty year perspective," *Journal of College Student Development*, 35 (January): 5–10.

17 Shaffer, H. B., 1966, "Cheating in school," *Editorial Research Reports*, 1 (May 11): 343–58, p. 343.

18 Schab, Fred, 1991, "Schooling without learning: Thirty years of cheating in high school," *Adolescence*, 26(104): 839–47.
19 Ibid.
20 Brandes, Barbara, 1986, "Academic honesty: A special study of California Students," Sacramento: California State Department of Education. ERIC Reproduction Document 272533.
21 Benton, Joshua and Hacker, Holly K., 2007 (June 4), "Efforts to stop TAKS cheating often fall short," *Dallas News*. Retrieved November 29, 2008 from www.dallasnews.com
22 McCabe, D. L., & Trevino, L. K., 1996, "What we know about cheating in college: Longitudinal trends and recent developments," *Change* (January/February): 29–33.
23 Bertram Gallant, 2008.
24 www.josephsoninstitute.org/Survey2004/2004reportcard_pressrelease.htm
25 http://www.josephsoninstitute.org/pdf/ReportCard_press-release_2006-1013.pdf
26 http://charactercounts.org/programs/reportcard/index.html
27 www.josephsoninstitute.org/Survey2004/2004reportcard_pressrelease.htm
28 These are classes for the more intellectually astute and university-bound students. When students take Advance Placement examinations, they earn extra points toward a grade point average. Therefore, an educated student can actually enter college or university with a better-than-perfect (4.0) grade point average. Advanced Placement exams are recognized in more than 60 countries outside the United States. See www.collegeboard.com for more information.
29 Pytel, 2007.
30 McCabe, 2005.
31 Stothard, Michael, 2008 (October 31), "'1 in 2' admits to plagiarism," *Varsity*. Retrieved October 31, 2008 from www.varsity.co.uk
32 Rocha, Maria Fátima & Teixeira, Aurora, A. C., 2006, "A cross-country evaluation of cheating in academia: Is it related to 'real world' business ethics?" FEP Working Papers, Research-Work in Progress-n. 214.
33 Lupton, Robert, A., & Chapman, Kenneth, J., 2002, "Russian and American college students' attitudes, perceptions and tendencies towards cheating," *Educational Research*, 44(1): 17–27.
34 Rocha & Teixeira, 2006.

35 Bertram Gallant, T., 2006, "Reconsidering academic misconduct as a complex organizational problem." Unpublished dissertation.
36 Bertram Gallant, 2008.
37 Ibid.
38 See the various citation guidelines for more information, e.g., the *American Psychological Association Manual* (5th edn) and *Modern Language Association Guide*.
39 Barr, R. B., & Tagg, J., 1994, "From teaching to learning – A new paradigm for undergraduate education," *Change* (November/December): 13–25.
40 Medina, Jennifer, 2008, "Next question: Can students be paid to excel?" *The New York Times*. Retrieved March 5, 2008.
41 Hallak, Jacques, & Poisson, Muriel, 2007, *Corrupt Schools, Corrupt Universities: What Can be Done?* Paris: International Institute for Educational Planning.
42 McCabe, 2005.
43 McCabe, 2005.
44 See, for example, Tapscott, D., 1998, *Growing Up Digital: The Rise of the Net Generation*. New York: McGraw-Hill; Duderstadt, J. J., Atkins, D. E., & Van Houweling, D., 2002, *Postsecondary Education in the Digital Age: Technology Issues and Strategies for American Colleges and Universities*, Westport, CG: Praeger.
45 Strom, P. S., & Strom, R. D., 2007, "Cheating in middle school and high school," *The Educational Forum*, 71 (Winter): 104–16 (p. 105).
46 Diekhoff, G. M., LaBeff, E. E., Clark, R. E., Williams, L. E., Francis, B., & Haines, V. J., 1996, "College cheating: Ten years later," *Research in Postsecondary Education*, 37(4): 487–502; Evans, E. D., & Craig, D., 1990, "Teacher and student perceptions of academic cheating in middle and senior high schools," *Journal of Educational Research*, 84(1): 44–52; Murdock, Tamera, B., Miller, Angela, & Kohlhardt, Julie, 2004, "Effects of classroom context variables on high school students' judgments of the acceptability and likelihood of cheating," *Journal of Educational Psychology*, 96(4): 765–77; Stephens, Jason, 2004, "Justice or just us? What to do about cheating?" Carnegie Perspectives: A different way to think about teaching and learning. Retrieved April 2, 2008 from www.carnegiefoundation.org/perspectives.
47 Hinman, Lawrence, M., 2005, "Virtual values: Reflections on academic integrity in the age of the internet," in Robert J. Cavalier (ed.), *The Impact*

of the Internet on our Moral Lives, Albany, NY: State University of New York Press, pp. 49–68 (p. 59).

48 Baron, Julie & Crooks, Steven M., 2005, "Academic integrity in web-based distance education," *Tech/Trends*, 49(2): 40–5; Heberling, M., 2002 (Spring), "Maintaining academic integrity in online education," *Online Journal of Distance Learning Administration*, 5(1). Retrieved February 19, 2008 from http://www.westga.edu/~distance/ojdla/

49 Ibid.

50 Varvel, Virgil, E. Jr., 2005, "Honesty in online education," *Pointers & Clickers: ION's Technology Tip of the Month*, 6(1): 1–20.

51 Amsden, D., 1977, "Fraud in academe," *Phi Kappa Phi Journal*, 57(1): 37–44.

52 Epstein, Max, A., 2003, *Combating Academic Fraud: Towards a Culture of Integrity*, Paris: International Institute for Educational Planning; Hallak & Poisson, 2007.

53 Ibid.; Braxton, J. M., & Bayer, A. E., 1999, *Faculty Misconduct in Collegiate Teaching*, Baltimore: Johns Hopkins University Press; Louis, K. S., Anderson, M. S., & Rosenberg, L., 1995, "Academic misconduct and values: The department's influence," *The Review of Postsecondary Education*, 18(4): 393–422; Rhoades, L. J., 2004, "New institutional research misconduct activity: 1992–2001." Retrieved November 26, 2007 from http://ori.dhhs.gov/misconduct/documents.

54 Plafker, Ted, 2002 (October 15), "Cheating on international exams also said to be widespread: In China, flood of fake diplomas," *International Herald Tribune*. Retrieved November 20, 2008, from www.iht.com

55 Anglen, R., 2006 (October 15), "College leaders' trips scrutinized – pricey hotels, meals common; Mesa community defends global outreach efforts," *Arizona Republic*. Retrieved March 15, 2007, from www. newsbank.com; Fain, Paul, 2008 (April 24), "West Virginia U bent rules to protect governor's daughter, panel says," *The Chronicle of Higher Education*. Retrieved April 24, 2008 from www.chronicle.com; Field, K., 2007 (May 15), "University of Texas at Austin fires financial-aid director implicated in student-loan scandal," *The Chronicle of Higher Education*. Retrieved May 15, 2007, from www.chronicle.com; Hallak & Poisson, 2007; Lederman, D., 2006 (November 9), "Southern Illinois chancellor forced out," *Inside Higher Education*. Retrieved November 9, 2006, from www.insidehighered.com; Su, E. Y.,

& Magee, M., 2007 (December 12), "Audit turns acclaim into outrage at Preuss," *Union-Tribune*. Retrieved December 19, 2007, from signonsandiego.com.

Chapter 3   Reasons for Academic Dishonesty

1   Drake, C. A., 1941, "Why students cheat," *Journal of Higher Education*, 12(4): 418–20.
2   Ibid., p. 420.
3   Schab, F., 1969, "Cheating in high school: Differences between the sexes," *Journal of the National Association of Women Deans and Counselors*, 33(1): 39–42.
4   Ludeman, W. W., 1938, "A study of cheating in public schools," *American School Boards Journal*, 96(1): 45–6.
5   Davis, S. F., Grover, C. A., Becker, A. H., & McGregor, L. N., 1992, "Academic dishonesty: Prevalence, determinants, techniques, and punishments," *Teaching of Psychology*, 19(1): 16–20.
6   Schab, 1969.
7   Davis et al., 1992.
8   Evans, E, D., & Craig, D., 1990, "Adolescent cognitions for academic cheating as a function of grade level and achievement status," *Journal of Adolescent Research*, 5(4): 325–45.
9   Haines, V. J., Diekhoff, G. M., LaBeff, E. E., & Clark, R. E., 1986, "College cheating: Immaturity, lack of commitment, and the neutralizing attitude," *Research in Higher Education*, 25(4): 342–54.
10   Baird, J. S., Jr., 1980, "Current trends in college cheating," *Psychology in the Schools*, 17(4): 515–22.
11   Heller, Donald, E., 2003, "The policy shift in state financial aid programs," in John Smart (ed.), *Higher Education: Handbook of Theory and Research* (Vol. XVII), New York: Springer, pp. 221–62.
12   Davis et al., 1992.
13   Cizek, G. J., 1999, *Cheating on Tests: How to Do It, Detect It, and Prevent It*, Mahwah, NJ: Lawrence Erlbaum Associates.
14   Kelly, J. A., & Worrell, L., 1978, "Personality characteristics, parent behaviors, and sex of the subject in relation to cheating," *Journal of Research in Personality*, 12(3): 179–88.

15 Karabenick, S. A., & Srull, T. K., 1978, "Effects of personality and situational variation in locus of control on cheating: Determinants of the 'congruence effect,'" *Journal of Personality*, 46(2): 72–95.

16 Johnson, C. D., & Gormly, J., 1971, "Achievement, sociability and task importance in relation to academic cheating," *Psychological Reports*, 28(3): 302.

17 Eisenberger, R., & Shank, D. M., 1985, "Personal work ethic and effort training affect cheating," *Journal of Personality and Social Psychology*, 49(4): 520–8.

18 Leming, J. S., 1978, "Cheating behavior, situational influence, and moral development," *Journal of Educational Research*, 71(3): 214–17.

19 Bruggeman, E. L., & Hart, K. J., 1996, "Cheating, lying, and moral reasoning by religious and secular high school students," *Journal of Educational Research*, 89(4): 340–4.

20 Huss, M. T., Curnyn, J. P., Roberts, S. L., Davis, S. F., Yandell, L., & Giordano, P., 1993, "Hard driven but not dishonest: Cheating and the Type A personality," *Bulletin of the Psychonomic Society*, 31(6): 429–30.

21 Weiss, J., Gilbert, K., Giordano, P., & Davis, S. F., 1993, "Academic dishonesty, Type A behavior, and classroom orientation," *Bulletin of the Psychonomic Society*, 31(3): 101–2.

22 Millham, J., 1974, "Two components of need for approval score and their relationship to cheating following success and failure," *Journal of Research in Personality*, 8(4): 378–92.

23 Corcoran, K. J., & Rotter, J. B., 1987, "Morality-Conscience-Guilt scale as a predictor of ethical behavior in a cheating situation among college females," *Journal of General Psychology*, 43(4): 344–9.

24 This information is taken from the annual survey of freshman students at four-year institutions, which has been conducted since 1966 by the Higher Education Research Institute (HERI) at the University of California at Los Angeles. See Rhodes, Frank H. T., 2006 (November 24), "After 40 years of growth and change, higher education faces new challenges," *The Chronicle of Higher Education*. Retrieved November 25, 2008 from www.chronicle.com. For more information on the work at HERI, visit http://www.gseis.ucla.edu/heri/index.php

25 Retrieved from http://responsibilityproject.com

Chapter 4   From Cheat Sheet to Text Messaging

1   *Tyler Morning Telegraph*, Tyler, TX, June 4, 2007, p. 1A, V. 77, #173.
2   Ibid., p. 1A.
3   *Tyler Morning Telegraph*, Tyler, TX, June 10, 2007, p. 3A, V. 77, #181.
4   Perhaps even more disturbing is the parents' outrage over the discipline their children would be facing for their crime. There were multiple stories about this in the news. See for example: Schweitzer, Sarah, 2007 (September 19), "School cheating scandal divides N.H. town," *The Boston Globe*; Dorning, Anne-Marie, 2007 (September 20), "Is cheating such a crime?" *ABC News*.
5   *Tyler Morning Telegraph*, Tyler, TX, February 27, 2008, p. 6B, V. 77, #58.
6   Davis, S. F., Grover, C. A., Becker, A. H., & McGregor, L. N., 1992, "Academic dishonesty: Prevalence, determinants, techniques, and punishments," *Teaching of Psychology*, 19(1): 16–20.
7   Davis, Grover, Becker, & McGregor, 1992.
8   http://search.1millionpapers.com/cgi-bin/query?mss=1millionpapers&q=Academic%20Dishonesty (retrieved Oct. 6, 2008).

Chapter 5   Short-Term Deterrents

1   Cizek, G. J., 1999, *Cheating on Tests: How to Do It, Detect it, and Prevent It*, Mahwah, NJ: Lawrence Erlbaum.
2   Mehrens, W. A., & Lehmann, I. J., 1991, *Measurement and Evaluation in Education and Psychology* (4th ed.), Fort Worth, TX: Holt, Rinehart and Winston.
3   Holland, P. W., 1996, *Assessing Unusual Agreement between the Incorrect Answers of Two Examinees using the K-index: Statistical Theory and Empirical Support* (ETS Technical Report No. 96–4), Princeton, NJ: Educational Testing Service.
4   Cizek, 1999.
5   Grijalva, T., Kerkvliet, J., & Nowell, C., 2003, "Academic honesty in online classes." Retrieved 15, 2008 from www.oregonstate.edu/dept/econ/pdf/cheat.online.pap6.pdf/

6   Stuber-McEwen, D., & Wiseley, P., 2008 (April), *Point, click, and cheat: Frequency and type of academic dishonesty in the virtual classroom.* Poster presented at the annual meeting of the Southwestern Psychological Association, Kansas City, MO.

7   Aaron, R. M., & Georgia, R. T., 1994, "Administrator perceptions of student academic dishonesty in collegiate institutions," *NASPA Journal*, 31(2): 83–91.

8   Murray, B., 1996 (January), "Are professors turning a blind eye to cheating?" *APA Monitor*: 1, 42.

9   Fishbein, L., 1994, "We can curb college cheating," *Education Digest*, 59(1): 58–61; Haines, V. J., Diekhoff, G. M., LaBeff, E. E., & Clark, R. E., 1986, "College cheating: Immaturity, lack of commitment, and the neutralizing attitude," *Research in Higher Education*, 25(4): 342–54; Singhal, A. C., 1982, "Factors in students' dishonesty," *Psychological Reports*, 51(6): 775–80.

10 Singhal, 1982.

11 Davis, S. F., Grover, C. A., Becker, A. H., & McGregor, L. N., 1992, "Academic dishonesty: Prevalence, determinants, techniques, and punishments," *Teaching of Psychology*, 19(1): 16–20.

12 Davis, Grover, Becker, & McGregor, 1992.

13 Stuber-McEwen & Wiseley, 2008.

14 Stuber-McEwen & Wiseley, 2008.

Chapter 6   Long-Term Deterrents

1   Pope, Denise, 2001, *Doing School: How We are Creating a Generation of Stressed-out, Materialistic, and Miseducated Students*, New Haven, CT: Yale University Press.

2   Michaels, James W., & Meithe, Terance, D., 1989, "Applying theories of deviance to academic cheating," *Social Science Quarterly*, 70(4): 870–5 (p. 882).

3   Eisenberg, Jacob, 2004, "To cheat or not to cheat: effects of moral perspective and situational variables on students' attitudes," *Journal of Moral Education*, 33(2): 163–78 (p. 176).

4   Pinker, Steven, 2008, "The Moral Instinct," *The New York Times Magazine*, January 13, p. 34.

5   See, for example, Tilly, Charles, 2008, *Credit and Blame*, Princeton: Princeton University Press.
6   Turck, James, F., 2003 (September 3), "The education crisis: Part 1. The real truth: A magazine restoring plain understanding." Retrieved December, 11, 2008, from http://www.realtruth.org/articles/156-aec.html
7   Kibler, William, L, Nuss, Elizabeth, M., Paterson, Brent, G., & Pavela, Gary, 1988, *Academic Integrity and Student Development: Legal Issues and Policy Perspectives*, Asheville, NC: College Administration Publications.
8   Nuss, Elizabeth, M., 1988, "Student development perspectives on academic integrity," in W. L. Kibler, E. M. Nuss, B. G. Paterson, & G. Pavela (eds), *Academic Integrity and Student Development: Legal Issues and Policy Perspectives*. Asheville, NC: College Administration Publications, pp. 7–18 (p. 9).
9   Ibid; Rest, J. R., 1985, "Evaluating moral development," in Jon Dalton (ed.), *Promoting Values Development in College Students*. NASPA Monograph Series, vol. 4, pp. 77–90.
10   Bloom, Paul, "First Person Plural," *The Atlantic Monthly* (November 2008), p. 92.
11   Ibid., p. 94.
12   Ibid.
13   Ibid., p. 96.
14   Ibid.
15   Ibid., p. 97.
16   Eisenberg, Jacob, 2004, "To cheat or not to cheat: effects of moral perspective and situational variables on students' attitudes," *Journal of Moral Education*, 33(2): 163–78 (p. 165).
17   Bertram Gallant's (2008) work, *Academic Integrity in the Twenty-First Century: A Teaching and Learning Imperative*, San Francisco: Jossey-Bass, is one exception to this although even she does not address the complexity of the issue from a moral development or moral dilemma perspective. Drinan, P., 1999, "Loyalty, learning and academic integrity," *Liberal Education*, 99(85): 28–33, is another exception as he tackles the ethical dilemma of loyalty to the school versus loyalty to one's friend or peer group.
18   Though this has been known to happen; consider the 2008 incident at a San Diego county high school: www.nctimes.com/articles/2008/04/30/news/inland/rb/nct5287d265bc1f8b758825743a00570.txt

19 Pinker, 2008, p. 56.

20 Eisenberg, 2004, p. 174.

21 Dalton, Jon, & Crosby, Pamela, 2008, "Challenging college students to learn in campus cultures of comfort, convenience and complacency," *Journal of College & Character*, 9(3): 1–5 (p. 2).

22 Ibid.

23 Austin, Zubin, Simpson, Stephanie, & Reynen, Emily, 2005, " 'The fault lies not in our students, but in ourselves': Academic honesty and moral development in health professions education – results of a pilot study in Canadian pharmacy," *Teaching in Higher Education*, 10(2): 143–56 (p. 154).

24 Nuss, 1988, p. 17.

25 University of Maryland, Kansas State University and St Mary's College of California are just three examples. Although the content and format of these seminars vary tremendously across contexts, they all focus on student ethical/integrity development and education. Tricia has experienced students coming through the Academic Integrity Seminar at UCSD, wanting to do more to educate the general student body about academic integrity. So, the potential of these seminars is not just individual development of the participants, but the stimulation of greater student involvement in integrity culture creation. We do, however, lack empirical data on the effectiveness of these seminars.

26 Eisenberg, 2004, p. 173.

27 Brody, Jane E., 2007 (December 18), "Teenage risks, and how to avoid them," *The New York Times*.

28 Bertram Gallant, Tricia, & Drinan, Patrick, 2006, "Institutionalizing academic integrity: administrator perceptions and institutional actions," *NASPA Journal*, 43 (4): 61–81; Bertram Gallant, Tricia, & Drinan, Patrick, 2008a, "Toward a model of academic integrity institutionalization: Informing practice in postsecondary education," *Canadian Journal of Higher Education*, 38(2): 25–44.

29 Bertram Gallant & Drinan, 2008a.

30 Levine, Michael, 2003, *A Branded World*, Hoboken, NJ: Wiley; Salzman, Marian, & Matahia, Ira, 2006, *Next Now: Trends for the Future*, New York: Palgrave Macmillan; Toma, J. Douglas, Dubrow, Greg, & Hartley, Matthew, 2005, "The uses of institutional culture: strengthening identification and building brand equity in higher education," *ASHE Higher Education Report*, 31(2): 1–105.

31 Toma et al., 2005, p. 28.

32 Marks, Denton, 2002, "Academic standards as public goods and varieties of free-rider behavior," *Education Economics*, 10(2): 145–63.

33 Salzman and Matahia, 2006.

34 Ibid.

35 Toma et al., 2005.

36 Ibid., p. 34.

37 Bensimon, Estela M., 2004, "The diversity scorecard: A learning approach to institutional change," *Change* (January/February): 45–52.

38 http://www.aashe.org/stars/

39 Drinan, Patrick, & Bertram Gallant, T., 2008, "Academic integrity: models, case studies, and strategies," in James M. Lancaster and Diane M. Waryold (eds.), *Student Conduct Practice: The Complete Guide for Student Affairs Professionals*, Sterling, VA: Stylus, pp. 258–78.

40 Toma et al., 2005, p. 34.

41 Mecklenburg, Gary, A., 2005, "Branding and organizational culture," in Alice M. Tybout and Tim Calkins (eds.), *Kellogg on Branding: The Marketing Faculty of the Kellogg School of Management*, Hoboken, NJ: Wiley & Sons, pp. 304–11 (p. 304).

42 Kibler, W. L., 1993, "A framework for addressing academic dishonesty from a student development perspective," *NASPA Journal*, 31(1): 8–18.

43 Bruhn, John G., Zajac, Gary, Al-Kazemi, Ali A., and Prescott Jr., Loren D., 2002, "Moral positions and academic conduct: parameters of tolerance for ethics failure," *Journal of Higher Education*, 73(4): 461–93 (p. 463).

44 There are researchers and academics who have argued for a professional code of ethics for the teaching profession. For example, Braxton, J. M., & Bayer, A. E., 2004, "Toward a code of conduct for undergraduate teaching," in J. M. Braxton and A. E. Bayer (eds.), *Addressing Faculty and Student Classroom Improprieties*, San Francisco: Jossey-Bass, pp. 47–55.

45 Ibid., p. 478.

46 Bertram Gallant & Drinan, 2008a, p. 26.

47 Bertram Gallant, 2006.

48 King, Patricia, M. & Mayhew, Matthew, J., 2002, "Moral judgment development in higher education: Insights from the defining issues test," *Journal of Moral Education*, 31(3): 247–70 (p. 252).

Chapter 7 The Call for Action and Wisdom

1 Wheatley, Margaret, J., 2002, *Turning to One Another: Simple Conversations to Restore Hope to the Future*, San Francisco: Berrett-Koehler, pp. 26–7.
2 Ibid., p. 3.
3 Friedman, Benjamin M., 2005, *The Moral Consequences of Economic Growth*, New York: Knopf, p. 51.
4 Ibid., p. 41.
5 Boyer, Ernest L., 1990, *Scholarship Reconsidered*, Princeton, NJ: Princeton University Press.
6 Bertram Gallant, 2008, *Academic Integrity in the Twenty-First Century: A Teaching and Learning Imperative*, San Francisco: Jossey-Bass.
7 Friedman, p. 17.
8 Kandel, Eric R., 2006, *In Search of Memory*, New York: W. W. Norton.

Chapter 8 Refining Our Tactics and Strategies

1 Brooks, David, 2007 (July 22), "The culture of debt," *New York Times*.
2 See, in particular, the February 2003 edition of the *IB World: The Magazine of the International Baccalaureate Organization* which dedicated a significant amount of space to "learning to learn honestly." The magazine can be viewed at www.ibo.org.
3 Gasser, Urs, 2008 (October 2). As cited in A. Guess's "Understanding students who were born digital," *InsideHigherEd*. Retrieved October 2, 2008 from www.insidehighered.com.
4 Pope, Justin, 2007 (June 3), "Theme of dishonesty runs beneath recent college headlines," *North County Times* (G1-G3).
5 Callahan, David, 2007, "Epilogue: Moving an integrity agenda," in E. Anderman, and T. Murdock (2006), *Psychology of Academic Cheating*, Burlington, MA: Elsevier Academic Press, pp. 313–17.
6 Thaler, Richard & Sunstein, Cass, 2008, *Nudge: Improving Decisions about Health, Wealth and Happiness*, New Haven, CT: Yale University Press, p. 13.

Chapter 9   An Optimistic (and Provocative) Conclusion

1. Zakaria, Fareed, 2008, "The future of American power," *Foreign Affairs*, (May/June): 18–43.
2. Ibid., p. 32.
3. Ibid., p. 32.
4. Ibid., p. 33.
5. Dostoevsky, Fyodor, 2002, *The Grand Inquisitor*, New York: Continuum.
6. See Fallows, James M., 1989, *More Like Us: Making America Great Again*, Boston: Houghton Mifflin.
7. Campbell, Jeremy, 2001, *The Liar's Tale*, New York: W.W. Norton & Company, p. 17.
8. Ibid., p. 17.
9. Ibid., p. 15.
10. See Bloom, David Allan, 1987, *The Closing of the American Mind*, New York: Simon & Schuster.
11. Campbell, 2001, p. 16.
12. Machiavelli, Nicolò, 2002 (translated by James B. Atkinson and David Sices), *The Sweetness of Power*. Northern Illinois University Press, p. 87.
13. Ibid., p. 44.
14. Alinsky, Saul, 1971, *Rules for Radicals*, New York: Random House, p. 24.
15. Machiavelli, 2002, p. 44.
16 Alinsky, 1971, pp. 98–124.

Name Index

Name Index

236

Subject Index

Subject Index

labeling theory 101
laboratory reports, cheating in 47,
  93
  detection of 112
  short-term deterrents 112,
    125–6, 127
  techniques used 100–1
Lake Woebegone effect 20
leadership 28–30
learning 186–7, 188
  collaborative 48, 51, 53
  mission 25, 26, 29, 150, 163,
    185, 191
  opportunities 13
  oriented students 79
learning what's on a test ahead of
  time 55, 56, 58
Liar's Tale, The (Campbell) 213
libertarian paternalism 204
Liberty Mutual (Responsibility
  Project) 86
lies/lying 212–13, 214
lifestyle choices 132
lip balm technique 96
long-term deterrents 129, 131–2
  moral development 53, 133–6
looking at classmate's paper 90, 92,
  105
loyalty 27, 135, 137, 138, 141, 142

Macleans magazine 201
male-female differences
  (dispositional determinants)
  77–8
meaning, search for 209–13
memories, personal (cheating
  experiences) 186–8

men (dispositional determinants)
  77–8
mentors 62
Midwestern State University 72
miniature camera-pager technique
  98
miniature computers 98
"minor"cheating 11
Mississippi State University 133
moderate cheating 54–5, 56–8
modest reform 189, 190–1
moral behavior 135, 138
moral conflict 134
*Moral Consequences of Economic
  Growth, The* (Friedman) 180
moral development 58, 168
  long-term deterrent 53, 133–66
  of teachers 152
  work ethic and 78
moral education 21–3, 25
"moral failings" 132
moral implication of intellectual
  growth 180–3
moral judgement 135, 136–7, 138
moral motivation 135, 137–8
moral reputation 145
moral sensitivity 135–6, 138
moral vocabulary 21–2, 25, 26, 28,
  29–30, 180, 193, 202
"moralization switch" 132
morally disagreeable behavior 42,
  47, 54, 62, 66, 132, 163
morally reprehensible behavior 44,
  47–8, 54, 62, 66, 91, 132, 148,
  163, 190, 209
morally responsible individuals 59
morals, changes in 81–7

Subject Index

Subject Index